Josephine Pollard

Ruth

A Bible heroine and other stories, told in the language of childhood

Josephine Pollard

Ruth
A Bible heroine and other stories, told in the language of childhood

ISBN/EAN: 9783337213893

Printed in Europe, USA, Canada, Australia, Japan

Cover: Foto ©Lupo / pixelio.de

More available books at **www.hansebooks.com**

DAVID & GOLIATH

Ruth, A Bible Heroine

AND OTHER STORIES

TOLD IN THE LANGUAGE OF CHILDHOOD

BY

Josephine Pollard

Author of BIBLE FOR YOUNG PEOPLE; HISTORY OF THE OLD TESTAMENT; HISTORY OF THE NEW TESTAMENT; BIBLE STORIES FOR CHILDREN; THE GOOD SAMARITAN; THE STORY OF JESUS; GOD MADE THE WORLD; THE BOYHOOD OF JESUS; SWEET STORIES OF GOD; *etc., etc.*

Illustrated

The Werner Company

NEW YORK   AKRON, OHIO   CHICAGO

1899

COPYRIGHT, 1899,
BY
THE WERNER COMPANY

Ruth,
A BIBLE HEROINE

RUTH, A BIBLE HEROINE

WHILE Is-ra-el was ruled by a judge whose name has not come down to us, a dearth came on the land of Ca-naan. And one of the Jews who dwelt in Beth-le-hem, took his wife and his two sons and went to stay for a while in the land of Mo-ab. His wife's name was Na-o-mi. The man died while they were in Mo-ab, and in a few years each of the sons took him a wife. And their names were Or-pah and Ruth. At the end of ten years the sons died, and Na-o-mi and their wives dwelt in the land of Mo-ab.

When Na-o-mi heard there was no lack of food in Is-ra-el, she made up her mind to go back to Beth-le-hem to live.

She told Or-pah and Ruth of her plan, and said if they choose to stay in the land of Mo-ab, where they were born, they might do so.

And they kissed her and wept and said they would go with her. But she bade them stay where they were, and at last Or-pah, with tears in her eyes, kissed Na-o-mi good-bye and went back to her own home. But Ruth would not leave her. She told Na-o-mi not to urge her to go, for nought but death should part them.

So they went to the town of Beth-le-hem where Na-o-mi used to live.

It was the days when the grain was ripe in the fields, and the men had gone out to cut it down.

And Na-o-mi had a kinsman in Beth-le-hem, whose name was Bo-az,

RUTH AND NA-O-MI.

and he was a rich and great man. And Ruth said to Na-o-mi, Let me now go to the fields and glean the ears of corn.

To glean is to pick up. And poor folks, who had no fields of their own, went to pick up that which was left on the ground for them.

RUTH.

And Na-o-mi told Ruth to go. And she went out and came to the field that was owned by the rich man, Bo-az.

When Bo-az saw Ruth he asked the men who she was, and where she came from. And one of them said, She came with Na-o-mi from the land of Mo-ab. And she said to us, I pray you let me glean where the field has been reaped. And we told her she might, and she has been there for some hours. Then Bo-az went to Ruth.

So she went out each day to his field, and gleaned there till the grain was all cut and in the barns.

Na-o-mi said to Ruth, Bo-az will win-now the

bar-ley to-night. To win-now is to fan, or to drive off by means of a wind. The grain was first threshed, then thrown from the hands up in the air. The wind would blow off the chaff and the good grain would fall to the ground.

Na-o-mi told Ruth to go in and speak to Bo-az the things she told her. So Ruth did as Na-o-mi said, and went down to the fields where Bo-az and his men were.

BO-AZ AND RUTH.

When she came back to Na-o-mi she told her all that she had said and done.

The next day Bo-az went down to the gate of

Beth-le-hem, and told all the chief men whom he met there that he meant to make Ruth his wife. And the men said they would make it known, and prayed the Lord would bless Ruth and add to the fame and wealth of the rich and great Bo-az.

So Bo-az took Ruth for his wife. And they had a son O-bed. And Na-o-mi was its nurse.

JOB

There was a man in the land of Uz whose name was Job. He was a good man and tried to do all that was right in the sight of the Lord. And God gave him ten chil-dren: sev-en boys and three girls. He gave Job great wealth, too, so that there was no man in all that part of the world as rich as he was.

When Job's sons were grown up and had homes of their own, they used to make feasts in turn, and send for their three sis-ters to come and eat and drink with them. And Job kept them in mind of all they owed to God, and urged them to lead good and true lives, and to do no wrong.

When Job had lived at his ease and been a rich man for a long term of years, a great change took place. He lost all his wealth, and all his chil-dren; for it was God's will to try him and see how he would bear these ills.

One day one of his men came to him in great haste, and said, While we were in the field with the ploughs, a band of thieves came and drove off the ox-en and ass-es and slew thy men who were with them, and I a-lone am left to tell thee.

While this man spoke, there came up one who said, A great fire has come down from the sky and burnt up thy sheep, and all those who took care of them, and I a-lone am left to tell thee.

While he yet spoke, a third man came and said, Thy foes came and took all thy cam-els, and slew the men who had charge of them, and I a-lone am left to tell thee.

Then a fourth came, and said, Thy chil-dren were at a feast in the house of thy first-born son, when there came a great wind that broke down the house, and it fell on the young men and they are all dead, and I a-lone am left to tell thee.

When Job heard these things he tore his clothes, and bowed down to the earth, as if at the feet of God. And he said, I had nought when I came in-to the world, and I shall have nought when I die and go out of it. God gave me all that I had, and God took it from me. He knows what is best for me and I thank him for all that he has done. So Job did not sin, nor speak ill of God, though his grief was so great and had come up-on him in such a strange, swift way.

To try Job still more, God let him get sick and he was in great pain. Boils came on him and from head to foot he was a mass of sores.

Then his wife came to Job and said, Dost thou still trust God? Do so no more, but curse him, though he kill thee for it.

Job said, Thou dost not speak wise words. When we have so much good from God, shall we not be con-tent to take our share of the ills he may send? In all this Job said not a word that was wrong.

Now Job had three friends, who, when they heard of his hard lot, came to talk with him and cheer him. But when they saw him, the change was so great they did not know him.

Then they rent their clothes and wept, and sat down on the ground near him, but did not speak for some time, for they could see that his grief was great. These friends thought that Job must have done some great sin, else these ills would not have been sent upon him. When they spoke to him they said, If thou hast done wrong, do so no more, and God will free thee from thy pains.

Now Job knew that he had done no wrong,

JOB, AND HIS FRIENDS.

and he said to them, You came to soothe me, but what you say does not soothe me at all. Did I send for you, or ask you to help me? If you were in such grief as I am, I might say hard things of you and call you bad men. But I would not do so; but would speak kind words to you, and try to help you bear your ills, and to make your grief less.

Then Job spoke of his own griefs, and said: O, that the Lord would put me to death that I might suf-fer no more. When I lie down at night I can-not sleep, but toss on my bed in pain and wish the day would dawn. Or, if I fall a-sleep for a while, I have the worst kind of dreams, so that I would be glad to die and wake no more in this world. O, that I had some one to speak to God for me, for he does not hear when I pray. Yet I know that he lives who will save my soul, and that he will come on the earth, and I shall rise up from my grave and see God for my-self.

But when Job found that he could not die, nor be made well, but must still bear his pains, he grew cross, and was not at all like the Job of old. He found fault, and said that his griefs were too great, and that God was not kind to put him in such pain.

His three friends did not try to calm him, or to cheer him with the hope that his woes would soon be at an end, nor did they bid him trust in God and seek help and strength from him. But they told him that he must have done some great wrong, else God would not have sent all these ills upon him.

This did not please Job, and he spoke to them in great wrath, and they spoke back in the same style.

When they had talked in this way for some time, and had each of them said things they ought not to have said, they heard a voice speak to them out of a whirl-wind that swept by the place. It was the voice of God.

And the voice spoke to Job and told him of the great works that God had done; that it was he who made the earth, the sea, and the sky. He sends the rain on the field to make the grass grow and the flowers to spring up. He sends the cold and the heat, the frost and the snow, and the ice that stops the flow of the streams. He sends the clouds, and the roar and the flash that come from them when the storms rage. He made the horse that is so swift and strong, and has no fear in time of war, but will rush in-to the fight at the sound of the trump.

All this and more the voice spoke from the whirl-wind. And when God had told Job of all these great works, he asked him if he could do these things, or if he thought he was so wise that he could teach God what it was best to do.

Then Job saw what a sin it was to find fault with

God. And he was full of shame, and said: My guilt is great; I spoke of that of which I knew naught, and I bow down in the dust before thee.

God said to Job's three friends, I am wroth with you, for you did not speak in the right way to Job. Now, lest I pun-ish you, take sev-en young bulls and sev-en rams and burn them on the al-tar, and ask Job to pray for you, for him will I hear. So they did as the Lord told them, and Job prayed for them, and God for-gave them their sins.

In a short time Job was well once more. His pains all left him; and then his friends and all his folks came to see him and they had a good feast. And each man brought him a rich gift, and the Lord blest him more than he had done before, and gave him twice as much wealth. He had great herds of sheep, and cam-els, and ox-en and ass-es, and large fields for them to roam in, and a host of men to care for them. So that he was a great man once more.

And God gave him ten chil-dren: sev-en boys and three girls. And when these girls grew up, there were no maids in all the land so fair as they in face and form. And Job had great peace of mind, and dwelt at his ease for long, long years; and when he died he was an old, old man.

SAMUEL, THE CHILD OF GOD

There was a man of Is-ra-el who went up each year from the town of Ra-mah to a place called Shi-loh to pay his vows to the Lord of hosts. And his wife, whose name was Han-nah, went with him. The man's name was El-ka-nah.

E-li was the high-priest at that time, and as he sat in the Lord's house he saw Han-nah on her knees with her eyes full of tears.

And he spoke to her in a kind voice, and said: May God grant thee what thou dost ask of

SAM-U-EL.

him. And Han-nah was glad at the high-priest's words, for she had asked God to give her a son.

And the Lord gave Han-nah a son, and she called his name Sam-u-el, which means "Asked of the Lord."

Sam-u-el was quite young when Han-nah took him up to the house of the Lord at Shi-loh. And when they brought the child to E-li, Han-nah said, I am the wo-man that stood by thee here and prayed to the Lord. For this child did I pray, and the Lord heard me and gave me what I asked for. So I have brought him to the Lord; so long as he lives shall he be the child of God. For this was the vow she made if God would give her a son.

And Sam-u-el was left to stay with E-li in the Lord's house.

Now E-li had two sons, and they were priests in the Lord's house. But they were not fit for the place, for they were bad men, and broke God's laws. And by their sins they kept men from the house of the Lord.

But Sam-u-el, though a young child, did what was right and pleased the Lord. And his moth-er made him a coat, and brought it to him each year when she and her hus-band went up to Shi-loh. And E-li spoke kind words to them, and asked the Lord to bless them for the sake of the child whom they gave to him.

Now E-li was an old man, and when he heard

of all the things his sons had done, he did not drive them out of the Lord's house as he should have done, but let them go on in their sins. He cared more to please his sons than he did to please the Lord.

One night when E-li and Sam-u-el lay down to sleep, the child heard a voice speak his name. And he said, Here am I. And he got up and ran to E-li, for he thought it was his voice, and he said, Here am I, for thou did'st call me.

E-li said, I did not call thee, my son. Go back, and lie down. And the lad did so.

In a short time he heard the same voice say, Sam-u-el—Sam-u-el.

And he rose at once and went to E-li, and said

HAN-NAH PRE-SENTS SAM-U-EL TO E-LI.

to him, Here am I, for thou did'st call me. But E-li said, I did not call thee, and sent the lad back to his bed once more.

Then Sam-u-el heard the voice a third time, and went to E-li and said, Here am I, for thou did'st call me.

And E-li knew it was the Lord who spoke to Sam-u-el. And he said to the lad, Go, lie down, and if he call thee, say, Speak, Lord, for I hear thee.

And Sam-u-el went and lay down. And the Lord came for the fourth time, and called, Sam-u-el —Sam-u-el!

And Sam-u-el said, Speak, Lord, for I hear thee.

And the Lord told Sam-u-el all that he meant to do to the house of E-li. He had let his sons go on in their sins, and they were to be put to death in a way that would make men fear God.

Sam-u-el lay still till day-light. Then he rose, but did not dare to tell E-li what God had told him.

But E-li called him and said, What did the Lord say to thee? I pray thee hide it not from me.

So Sam-u-el told E-li all that the Lord had said. When E-li heard it, he said, It is the Lord, let him do what he thinks is best.

And Sam-u-el grew, and the Lord was with him and blest him, and it was known to all that he was one of God's saints, who could fore-tell things that were to take place. Such wise men were some-times called seers.

The words which God spoke to Sam-u-el came

true; for the chil-dren of Is-ra-el went out to fight the Phil-is-tines, and a host of them were slain.

Those who came back said, Let us take the ark out with us to save us from our foes.

CAP-TURE OF THE ARK.

Now God had not told them to take the ark, and it was a sin for them to touch it. They should have put their trust in the Lord, and looked to him for help.

But they sent to Shi-loh for the ark, and E-li's two sons came with it. When it was brought to the camp the Jews gave such a shout that the earth shook with the noise.

And when the Phil-is-tines heard it, they said, What does it mean? And they were told that the ark of the Lord had been brought to the camp of Is-ra-el.

And they were in great fear; for they said, God is come to the camp! Woe un-to us, for this is the first time such a thing has been done!

And they said, Let us be strong and fight like men, that we may not be slaves to these Jews!

So they fought once more with the Jews, and slew a host of them, and the rest fled to their tents. And the ark of the Lord fell in-to the hands of the foe, and E-li's two sons were slain.

And the same day a man ran down to Shi-loh, with his clothes rent, and bits of earth on his head to show his grief.

E-li sat on a seat by the way-side, where he kept watch, for he was in great fear lest harm should come to the ark of God. And when the man came through the crowd and told that the ark was lost, all cried out with great fear. And when E-li heard the noise, he said, What is it? What do those sounds mean? For his eyes were dim with age, and he could not see.

And the man ran up to E-li and said, I am he

that came out of the fight, and I fled from there to-day.

And E-li said, What word hast thou, my son?

THE RE-TURN OF THE ARK.

And he said that Is-ra-el had been put to flight with great loss, his two sons were dead, and the ark of God in the hands of the Phil-is-tines.

When the man spoke of the ark of God, E-li fell off

the seat by the side of the gate, and broke his neck, and died there. And he had been a high priest and a judge in Is-ra-el for two-score years.

And the ark of God was with the Phil-is-tines for more than half the year, and to each place where it was sent it brought great grief.

So at last they sent for their wise men, and said to them, What shall we do with the ark of the Lord? To what place shall we send it?

And the wise men told them to make a new cart, and tie two cows to it, but to bring the calves home with them. Then they should put the ark on the cart, and let the cows draw it where they would.

If the cows should leave their calves and go down to the land of Is-ra-el, it would be a sign that the Lord was their guide, and that he had sent these ills on the Phil-is-tines for their great sins.

But if the cows did not take the ark, it would show that the Lord did not want it back, and that all these ills they had to bear had come by chance, and were not sent from the Lord.

So the Phil-is-tines did as their wise men said. They took the two cows and tied them to the cart, and shut up their calves at home. And they laid the ark on the cart, and let the cows go where they chose.

And the cows took the straight road to the land

of Is-ra-el till they came to a place called Beth-she-mesh.

The Jews who dwelt there were out in the wheat fields. And the cows brought the cart to the fields of a man named Josh-u-a, and stood there by a great stone.

Then some of the men of Le-vi came and took the ark and set it on the stone. And they broke up the cart, and burnt the cows as a gift of praise to the Lord.

SAMUEL, THE MAN OF GOD

When E-li died, Sam-u-el was made a judge in Is-ra-el. And he went from place to place to teach men the law. And as the ark had not been brought back to Shi-loh, Sam-u-el built an al-tar in his own house and served God there.

The chil-dren of Is-ra-el set up strange gods, and the Phil-is-tines went to war with them. And Sam-u-el told them to give up their false gods and serve the Lord, and he would save them from their foes. And they did so. And he said, Come up to Miz-peh, and I will pray to the Lord for you.

And they came to Miz-peh, and gave their hearts to the Lord, and were in grief for their sins.

And when the Phil-is-tines heard they were at Miz-peh, they went up to fight them. And the chil-dren of Is-ra-el were in great fear, and Sam-u-el plead for them, and when the fight came on the Lord sent a fierce storm that put the Phil-is-tines to flight, and they fled from the field with great loss.

And Sam-u-el set up a stone at Miz-peh, and gave it the name of Eb-en-e-zer—"The Stone of Help."

When Sam-u-el was an old man he set his two sons to judge Is-ra-el. But his sons were not just men, and did not rule as their fath-er had done. If a man did wrong, they would say it was right if he paid them for it. And the wise men came to Sam-u-el, and said to him, As thou art old, and thy sons walk not in thy ways, make us a king to judge us.

Sam-u-el felt hurt when they asked him to choose a king, and asked the Lord to tell him what to do.

And the Lord told Sam-u-el to choose a king for them.

Now there was a man whose name was Kish, and he had a son whose name was Saul, a tall young man of fine form and good looks.

And the ass-es of Kish were lost. And he said to Saul, his son, Take one of the men with you, and go find the ass-es.

Samuel, the Man of God.

And they went a long way and could not find them. And Saul said to the man with him, Come, let us go back, lest my fath-er think we are lost.

THE STONE OF HELP.

And the man said to Saul, There is a man of God here, and what he says is sure to come to pass. It may be that he can tell us what we ought to do

Saul said, Thy word is good; come, let us go. And they went to the town where Sam-u-el, the man of God, was. And they met him on their way.

And the Lord made it known to Sam-u-el that this was the man he should choose to reign in Is-ra-el.

And Saul drew near to Sam-u-el, and said, Tell me, I pray thee, where the seer's house is.

And Sam-u-el said, I am the seer; and the ass-es that were lost are found. And he took Saul and his man to his own house, and made them spend the night there.

The next day Sam-u-el took Saul to the roof of his house, and had a talk with him.

Then they went out on the street, and as they drew near the gate of the town, Sam-u-el said to Saul, Bid thy man pass on, but do thou stand still for a while, that I may show thee the word of God.

Then Sam-u-el took a horn of oil and poured it on Saul's head.

This was done when a man was made a high-priest; and the same thing was done when he was made a king. And God was pleased with Saul, and gave him a new heart; but as yet none but these two knew that Saul was to be King of the Jews.

Sam-u-el spoke to the chil-dren of Is-ra-el and told them once more all that the Lord had done for them, how he had brought them out of the land of

E-gypt, and set them free from their foes, and yet they would not serve the Lord, but cried out for a king. So he bade them all go up to Miz-peh that the Lord might choose them a king.

And the Lord chose Saul. But when the men went to seek for him, they could not find him. And the Lord said, He hath hid in the midst of the stuff. And they ran and brought him out, and he was so tall that all the rest had to look up to him.

SAUL IN HIS HID-ING PLACE.

And Sam-u-el said, This is he whom the Lord hath sent to rule thee. There is none like him, as thou canst see.

And they all cried out, God save the king! Then Sam-u-el told them what they were to do, and how the king was to rule, and wrote it down in a book.

When Saul had been king for two years, he set out with his son, Jon-a-than, to fight the Phil-is-tines. And a great host went with them. And the Phil-is-tines had more men than they could count. And when the Jews saw the strength of their foes, they were in great fear, and ran and hid in caves and pits, or fled to the high hills where the rocks would screen them. So there were but few left to go out with Saul, and they shook with dread.

And Saul came to Gil-gal, where he was to meet Sam-u-el, but he was not there. Sam-u-el had told him to wait for him, and he would tell him what he was to do.

But at the end of a week Saul had the flesh brought to him and laid on the stone, and he set fire to it, that the flame might rise to God and bring peace to the land. And as soon as Saul had done this thing, Sam-u-el came. And Saul went out to meet him, that he might bless him.

And Sam-u-el said, What hast thou done?

And Saul told of the strait he was in, and that the Phil-is-tines were near in great force, and said that when Sam-u-el did not come he felt that he must send up a plea to God for aid in this hour.

Sam-u-el told him that he had done wrong.

When the Lord told him to wait, he should wait. And now his reign would be a short one, and God would choose a new king to take his place.

In those days men fought with bows and ar-rows. And while the Jews were held as slaves by the Phil-is-tines they would not let them have swords or spears, lest they should rise up and kill them.

And they sent all the smiths out of the land, lest they should make these things for the chil-dren of Is-ra-el.

So when they went out to fight none of them had a sword or a spear but Saul and his son.

In those days men wore coats of mail, and bore a shield with them so as to ward off the darts. These shields were made of a thick piece of wood, on which the skin of an ox was stretched when dried.

Jon-a-than, Saul's son, wore a coat of mail, and had a man to bear his spear and his shield when he did not care to use them. And he said to his man, Come, let us go to the camp of the Phil-is-tines. For it may be that the Lord will help us.

And the man said he would go.

Jon-a-than said this should be their sign: They would go where the foe could see them, and if they said, Wait there till I come to you, they would know the Lord did not mean to help them. But if the Phil-is-tines said, Come up to us and we will show you some-thing, they would go up, for the Lord would be with them.

So Jon-a-than and his man stood out where the foe could see them. And the Phil-is-tines made sport of them, and cried out, Come up to us, and we will shew you some-thing.

And the two went up the rocks on their hands and feet, and fought with the Phil-is-tines, and slew a score of them. And the Lord shook the earth, so that the Phil-is-tines were in great fear.

Now Saul and the men who were with him did not know what his son had done. But his watch-man, who was on the look-out, saw that there was a fight in the camp of the Phil-is-tines, and told Saul of it.

And Saul and his men went to join in the fight. And all those who had hid in caves and holes, or up on the mount, when they heard that the Phil-is-tines had fled, went with Saul, and Is-ra-el won the day.

But Saul did not de-sire to please the Lord in all things. For when the Lord sent him out to fight King A-gag, he told Saul to wipe him and all he had from the face of the earth. But Saul kept back some of the spoils, the best of the sheep and lambs, and did not put the king to death as he should have done.

And the Lord told Sam-u-el that Saul was not a good king, and his reign should be short.

And it made Sam-u-el sad to hear this, and he prayed to God all night. Then he had a talk with Saul, who did not look at his sins in the right light. And Sam-u-el told him that his reign as king would soon be at an end.

God told Sam-u-el not to mourn for Saul, but to go down to Beth-le-hem, to the house of a man named Jes-se, one of whose sons was to be made king. And the Lord said he was not to look for one with a fine face or form. For the Lord sees not as man sees, and he looks on the heart.

DA-VID A-NOINT-ED BY SAM-U-EL.

So he went down to Beth-le-hem, and did as the Lord told him. And Jes-se had his sev-en sons pass one by one before Sam-u-el. And Sam-u-el thought that the first-born must be the one whom God chose to be king. But the Lord told him he was not the one. And they all went by, and not one of them was the one on whom God had set his seal.

And Sam-u-el said to Jes-se, Are these all thy sons?

And Jes-se said, No there is yet one left; but he is quite a lad, and is now in the field where he cares for the sheep.

And Sam-u-el told Jes-se to send for him at once. And Jes-se sent for him, and he was brought in, and his cheeks were red, and his eyes bright. And the Lord said to Sam-u-el, Rise—for this is he.

And Sam-u-el rose, and took the horn of oil and poured it on the young man's head. So the Lord chose Da-vid to be king when Saul should be put out of the way.

And Da-vid felt a great change in his heart, for the Lord was there to make him strong and wise, and fit for the high place he was to fill.

But there was no peace in Saul's heart, and his mind was ill at ease.

And his men said it might soothe him to have some one play on the harp. For sweet sounds will some-times calm the mind.

So Saul said, Find a man who can play well on the harp, and bring him to me.

And one of them said that he knew such a man. He was the son of Jes-se, who dwelt at Beth-le-hem, and his name was Da-vid.

And Saul sent men to Jes-se and told him to send Da-vid, his son, who kept the sheep.

And Da-vid came to Saul, and stayed with him to wait on him. And when Saul was sad and ill at ease, Da-vid would take his harp and play for him, and he would soon be well.

DAVID AND SAUL

While Saul was yet king, the Phil-is-tines came forth once more to fight the chil-dren of Is-ra-el. And Saul and his men went out to meet them. There were two high hills on each side of a deep vale, and from these two hills the foe-men fought.

The Phil-is-tines had on their side a man who was more than ten feet high. He wore a coat of mail, and was bound with brass from head to foot, so that no sword or spear could wound him.

And he cried out to Saul's men, Choose a man

from your midst and let him come down to me. If he can fight with me and kill me, then we will be your slaves. But if I kill him then you must serve us. I dare you to send a man to fight with me.

When Saul and his men heard these words they were in great fear, for there was no one in their ranks who would dare fight with such a gi-ant.

And each morn and eve, for more than a month, this great man, whose name was Go-li-ath, drew near Saul and his troops and dared them to send a man out to fight him.

Now when the war broke out three of Jes-se's sons went with Saul, but Da-vid went back to Beth-le-hem to feed sheep.

And Jes-se said to Da-vid, Take this parched corn and these ten loaves of bread, and run down to camp and bring me back word how thy broth-ers are.

And Da-vid rose up the next morn, and found some one to take care of his sheep, and went as his fath-er told him.

And he came to the camp just as the men were on their way to the fight, and the air was filled with their shouts.

And he left the goods he had brought in the care of a man, and ran in the midst of the troops, and spoke to his three broth-ers.

And while he stood there, Go-li-ath came out from the ranks of the Phil-is-tines, and dared some one to fight with him.

And Da-vid heard his words. And the men of Is-ra-el fled from his face. And Da-vid heard them speak of what would be done to the man who should kill him; for the king would give him great wealth, and set him in a high place.

And Da-vid spoke to the men near him, and made use of strong words.

And his brothers told him to go home and take care of his sheep, for it was just a trick of his to come up to camp that he might see the fight.

DA-VID BE-FORE SAUL.

Da-vid said, I have done no wrong? and the men to whom he spoke went and told Saul what he had said. And Saul sent for him, but did not know that he was the same one who used to play on the harp for him.

And Da-vid told Saul he would go out and fight the great man from Gath. And Saul said, Thou art but a youth, and he has been a man of war all his days.

Then Da-vid told Saul how he had fought with and slain the wild beasts that came out of the woods to eat up the lambs of his flock. And, said he, this man is no more than a wild beast, and the Lord will save me from him as he did from the paw of the li-on and the bear.

And Saul said, Go, and the Lord go with thee. And Saul put on him a coat of mail, and clothed him in brass from head to foot, and hung a sword at his side. But Da-vid took them all off, and said, I have not tried them, and can-not use them.

And he took his staff in his hand, and chose five smooth stones from the brook and put them in a bag that he wore. And his sling was in his hand when he drew near to Go-li-ath.

Go-li-ath came near to Da-vid, and when he saw what a youth he was, he drew up his head with great scorn.

Da-vid ran to meet him, and put his hand in his bag and drew forth a stone, and slung it, and struck Go-li-ath on the fore-head with such force that the

DA-VID WITH GO-LI-ATH'S HEAD.

stone sank in through the bone and he fell on his face to the earth.

Then Da-vid ran and stood on Go-li-ath, and drew his sword from its sheath, and slew him and cut off his head.

And when the Phil-is-tines saw that the man in whom they had put their trust was dead they fled.

And Da-vid came back from the fight with the head of Go-li-ath in his hand, and was brought to Saul.

And Saul would not let Da-vid go back to his own home, but made him stay with him. And Jon-a-than fell in love with him, and to show his love, took off all the rich clothes he had on and put them on Da-vid, and gave him his sword, his bow, and his belt. And Da-vid did as Saul told him, and all who saw him were pleased with him, and Saul put him at the head of his men of war.

But when King Saul and his men went through the towns on their way back from the fight, the folks came out and sang and danced to praise them for what they had done.

But they said more in praise of Da-vid than of Saul, and when Saul heard it he was wroth, and from that day ceased to be Da-vid's friend.

The next day Da-vid stood near Saul with his harp in his hand to play him some sweet tunes.

And Saul held a spear in his hand, and he cast it at Da-vid so that it would go through him and pin him to the wall. But Da-vid saw it and took a step one side, and it did him no harm.

Twice was this done, and when Saul found that he could not hurt Da-vid, he was in great fear of him, for he knew the Lord was with him. So he drove Da-vid from his house, and sent men to lay in wait to kill him.

But Da-vid fled from them and ran to the place where Jon-a-than was, and said to him, What have I done that the king seeks my life?

JON-A-THAN AND DA-VID.

Now Jon-a-than did not know that the king meant to kill Da-vid, so he said to him, Thou shalt not die.

My fath-er would have told me if he meant to kill thee. But Da-vid said it was true.

The next day was to be a feast day, and the king would look for Dav-id to come and eat with him. But Da-vid was in such fear of Saul that he did not care to go, and begged Jon-a-than to let him hide him-self for three days. If the king asks where I am, said Da-vid, tell him that thou did'st give me leave to go home.

Jon-a-than told Da-vid that at the end of the three days he should come and hide in the field near a rock that was there. And Jon-a-than said he would shoot three ar-rows as if he took aim at a mark. And he would send a lad out to pick them up. And if he said to the lad, Go, find them, they are on this side of thee, then Da-vid might know that all was at peace and the king would do him no harm. But if he should cry out that the darts were be-yond the lad, then Da-vid would know that he must flee, for the king meant to do him harm.

So Da-vid hid him-self in the field; and when the feast day came Saul sat down to eat with his back to the wall. And he saw that Da-vid was not in his place, but said not a word. The next day when he found Da-vid was not in his place, Saul said to his son, Why comes not Da-vid to eat these two days?

Jon-a-than said that Da-vid plead so hard for

David and Saul.

leave to go home to his own folks, that he had told him to go, and that was why he was not at the feast.

Then Saul was in a great rage, and said to his son, As long as Da-vid lives thou canst not be a king. Send for him, and bring him here that he may be put to death.

And Jon-a-than said, Why should he be slain? What hath he done?

Saul threw his spear at Jon-a-than. And the young man knew by this that the king meant to kill Da-vid.

JON-A-THAN SHOOT-ING THE AR-ROWS.

So the next morn the king's son went out to the field, and took a lad with him. And he said, Run now, and pick up the ar-rows that I shoot.

And as he ran, Jon-a-than sent a dart o'er his head; and when the lad came to the place where it fell, the king's son cried out, It is be-yond thee. Make haste, and stay not.

Da-vid heard these words and knew that he must flee, for if Saul caught him he would kill him.

The lad brought the darts to Jon-a-than, and did not know why the king's son had shot them and called out to him as he did. And Jon-a-than gave him his bow and ar-rows, and sent him back to town with them.

As soon as the lad was gone, Da-vid came out from the place where he was hid, and fell on his face to the ground, and bowed three times. Then he rose and threw his arms round Jon-a-than's neck, and the two friends wept as if their hearts would break.

Then Da-vid fled from Saul, and hid in the woods and caves.

Saul went out with a large force of men to seek Da-vid on the rocks where the wild goats fed. And Saul came to a cave, and went in to lie down and rest.

Da-vid and his men were in the cave, but Saul could not see them. And the men wished to kill Saul; but Da-vid would not let them. While he was there Da-vid stole up to Saul and cut off a piece of his robe. And Saul did not know it.

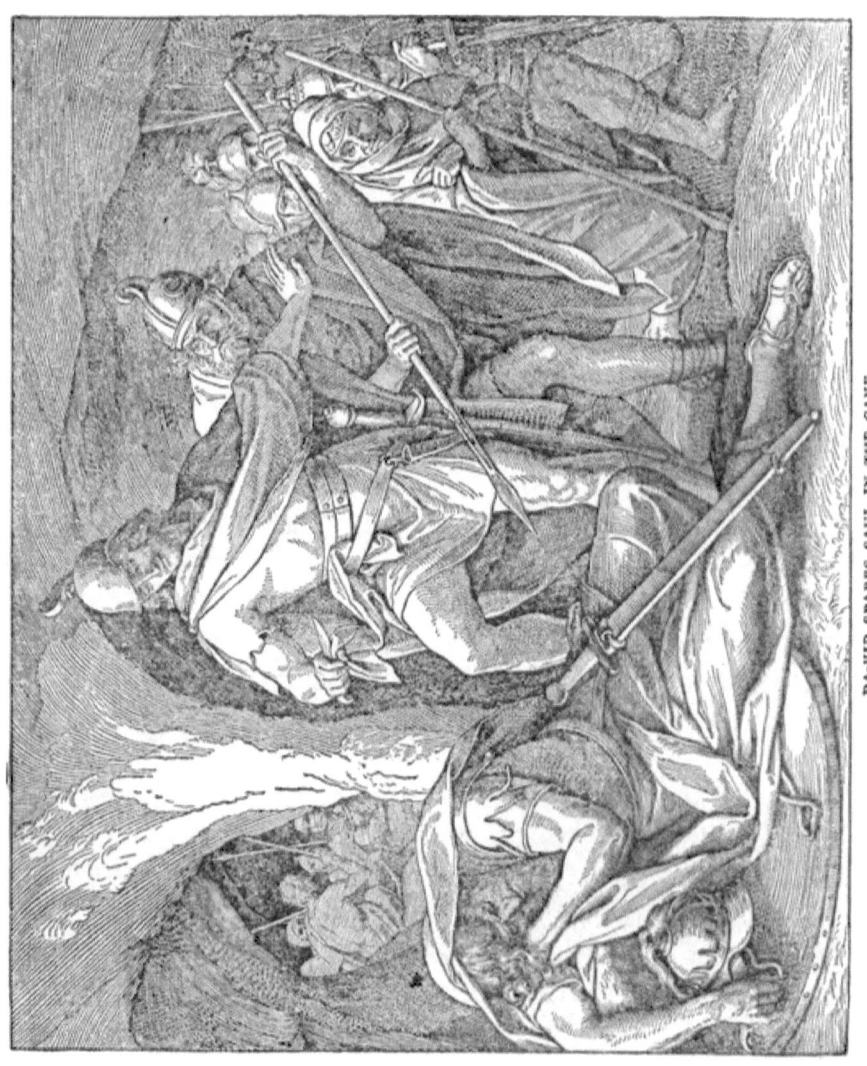

DAVID SPARES SAUL IN THE CAVE.

When Saul went out of the cave, Da-vid went out af-ter him and cried out, My lord and my king!

And when Saul looked back, Da-vid bowed down to him with his face to the earth. And he told Saul to pay no heed to those who said he meant to harm the king. For if he had sought to kill Saul he might have done so that day while he was in the cave. And Da-vid showed Saul the piece of his robe he had cut off.

And some bade me kill thee, said Da-vid, but I would not, for thou art my lord and my king. Then Da-vid held up the piece of cloth he had cut from Saul's robe, and said, Since I was so near thee as to cut this off and did not kill thee, thou may'st know that I have no wish to harm thee. Yet thou dost hunt for me to kill me. Let the Lord judge 'twixt thee and me, and save me from thy hand, and save thee as he will, for I will not harm thee.

When Saul heard Da-vid speak thus, all hate went out of his heart, and he wept as he said, Thou hast done good to me for the wrongs I did thee, and may the Lord bless thee for it. Now I know that thou wilt some day be the king of Is-ra-el.

And Saul went home, and Da-vid and his men went back to the cave.

But Da-vid knew that he could not trust Saul, so he fled to the land of the Phil-is-tines, and he and his men dwelt there in the town of Gath for the space of a year and four months.

While he was there, the Phil-is-tines went out to fight with Saul once more, and when he saw what a host of them there was, his heart shook with fear. He asked the Lord what he should do, but the Lord did not come to him in dreams, or speak one word to him.

Sam-u-el was dead, and the Lord had said it was a sin to go to a witch, or a seer, to find out the things that would take place, and Saul had sent all these folks out of the land.

DA-VID TAKES GO-LI-ATH'S SWORD.

But now he was in such a strait that he felt he must have help of some sort. And one of his men told him there was at En-dor a witch who could work strange charms, and fore-tell what was to take place. So the king drest him-self so that he would not be known, and went at night with two of his men to see the witch of En-dor. And he said to her, Bring me up him whom I shall name to thee.

And the witch said to him, Dost thou not know that Saul has sent all those that work charms out of the land? And why dost thou set a snare for my life, so that I will be put to death?

And Saul said, As the Lord lives there shall no harm come to thee for this thing.

Then the witch said, Whom shall I bring up to thee? And he said, Bring me Sam-u-el.

So the witch made strange signs and spoke strange words, and swept her wand round and round. And when she saw the form of Sam-u-el rise up, she cried with a loud voice, Why did'st thou not tell me the truth? for thou art Saul!

And the king said, Have no fear. What did'st thou see?

And the witch said, I saw an old man with a cloak round him.

And Saul knew it was Sam-u-el, and bowed his face to the ground. And Sam-u-el said, Why hast thou brought me up? And Saul told him that he was in a great strait, that God had left him, and did not come to him in dreams or by the hand of wise

SAUL CONSULTETH A WITCH AT EN-DOR.

Y. F. B.—12

SAUL'S DEATH.

men, and he thought that Sam-u-el might tell him what to do.

Sam-u-el said, Why then dost thou ask of me if the Lord hath left thee? He hath done to thee just as he said he would. Thy reign is at an end, and Da-vid shall rule in thy stead. And he told Saul that the next day he and his sons would be dead, and Is-ra-el in the hands of the foes.

When Saul heard these words he fell down in a swoon, for he had had no food for a day and a night.

And the witch brought bread and bade him eat, that he might have strength to go on his way. And Saul and his men ate of the food, and went their way that night.

Now the lords of the Phil-is-tines brought all their troops to a place called A-phek. And the king of Gath went there, and took Da-vid and his men with him. But the lords of the Phil-is-tines would not have the Jews in their midst lest they should turn on them and give them in-to the hands of king Saul.

So Da-vid and his men had to leave the camp, and the Phil-is-tines went out to fight, and the men of Is-ra-el fled from them with great loss. The king's three sons were slain, and an ar-row struck Saul and gave him a bad wound.

And Saul said to the man who bore his shield, Draw thy sword and put me to death. But the man did not dare to kill his king. So Saul took his own sword and fell on it, and thus died by his own hand. And when the man saw that Saul was dead, he fell on his sword and died with him.

And when it was known that Saul and his sons were dead, the Jews fled from that part of the land, and the Phil-is-tines went to live there.

In the course of a few years Da-vid was made king of Is-ra-el, and then went to live at Je-ru-sa-lem. He went to war, and took spoils of rich kings, and the Lord was with him, for he sought to do that which was right and just.

Da-vid had two sons: Sol-o-mon and Ab-sa-lom.

And in all the land there was no man with such a fine face and form as Ab-sa-lom, and he won much praise for his good looks. And he had a thick growth of long hair. But Ab-sa-lom had a bad heart, and his sins made Da-vid weep. But he did not scold Ab-sa-lom as he should have done, for the king was fond of his son, and so Ab-sa-lom went on from bad to worse.

He told what he would do when he was king, and made friends with those who thought it a fine thing to be on good terms with the king's son.

When he was two-score years of age, Ab-sa-lom said to the king, Let me, I pray thee, go up to Heb-ron to pay my vows.

David and Saul.

And Da-vid told him to go. But it was not to serve the Lord that Ab-sa-lom went, but to have him-self made king in-stead of Da-vid. And he took ten score men with him, who did not know why or where they went, and sent spies all through the land to speak in his praise and urge that he be made king.

And when Da-vid heard of it he said to his men, Rise, let us flee from this place, lest Ab-sa-lom come and put us to death.

And they all fled from Je-ru-sa-lem, and went to hide in some lone place. And when Ab-sa-lom came to Je-ru-sa-lem he

DA-VID FOR-GIV-ING AB-SA-LOM.

went to one of Da-vid's friends and asked him what he should do to be made king. A-hith-o-phel, who had once been a friend of Da-vid, and had now gone with the king's son, had said that he would go out with a large force and come up with Da-vid when he was weak and faint, so that he would be in a great fright. Those who were with Da-vid would flee, and he would soon put the king to death. Then, of course, Ab-sa-lom would be king.

But Ab-sa-lom would not do this till he had heard what Hu-sha-i said. Now Hu-sha-i was a true friend of Da-vid, and he told Ab-sa-lom to take more men than A-hith-o-phel had said, for he thought that would give Da-vid a chance to get out of the way. And Hu-sha-i sent two young men to tell Da-vid not to stop on the plains that night, but to cross the Jordan, lest he and all who were with him should be put to death.

But a boy saw the two sons of the high-priest who were on their way to Da-vid, and went and told Ab-sa-lom. And the priest's sons ran to a house near by, and hid in the well. And the woman who kept the house spread corn on top so that no one could see that a well was there.

And when Ab-sa-lom's men came up and asked the wo-man where the priest's sons were, she said they had gone on past the brook Ked-ron. And when the two could not be found the men went back.

Then the priest's sons came up out of the well, and made haste to give to Da-vid the word that Hu-sha-i had sent. And at dawn Da-vid and all his men crossed the Jor-dan.

As soon as Ab-sa-lom had all the men he thought he would need, he set out to fight with Da-vid. And Da-vid drew up his men in line, and put Jo-ab at their head. And the king said, I will go out with you. But the men said he should not; so Da-vid staid by the gate and saw them go out to the fight, and bade them be kind to Ab-sa-lom for his sake.

The fight took place in a wood. Ab-sa-lom rode on a mule, and as the mule passed 'neath a great oak, Ab-sa-lom's head caught in a branch, and he hung in mid air, while the mule went off down the road.

THE DEATH OF AB-SA-LOM.

And a man saw it and told Jo-ab. And Jo-ab said, Why did'st thou not kill him? And the man said he would not kill the king's son, for he had heard Da-vid ask them to be kind to him.

But Jo-ab said, I can-not waste time with thee. And he took three darts in his hand and thrust them through Ab-sa-lom, so that he died. And he was thrown in-to a pit that was in the wood, and a great heap of stones was piled on him. And all the men who had been with him went back to their tents.

Da-vid sat in the gate, and when men came back with news of the fight, he would ask of each one, Is Ab-sa-lom safe? And at last one of them said, May all the king's foes be as this young man is. Then Da-vid knew that Ab-sa-lom was dead, and he went to his own room and wept.

DA-VID HEAR-ING OF AB-SA-LOM'S DEATH.

And he cried out with a loud voice, O, my son, Ab-sa-lom; my son, my son Ab-sa-lom! I would that God had let me die in thy stead, O, Ab-sa-lom, my son, my son!

Da-vid was king for two-score years, and was an old man when he died and had hosts of friends. And when he felt that his death was near, he bade his men take Sol-o-mon to a place called Gi-hon, and pour oil on his head. Then they were to blow the horn and cry out, God save King Sol-o-mon.

And this was done; and when Da-vid died, Sol-o-mon sat on his throne and ruled Is-ra-el.

SOLOMON, THE WISE MAN

Sol-o-mon gave his heart to God when he was young, and tried to lead a good life, and to do no wrong. And God spoke to him in a dream one night and said, Ask what I shall give thee.

And Sol-o-mon said, Grant me, I pray thee a wise mind that I may know right from wrong, and judge well those who look up to me as their king.

This speech pleased the Lord, and he said, Since thou didst not ask me for great wealth, or for long life, or that thy foes might be put to death, I will make thee wise, and will give thee both great wealth and a long life if thou wilt serve me and keep my laws.

There came two wo-men to the king. And one of them said, My lord, I and this wo-men live in one house, and we each of us had a son. And this wo-man's child died in the night, and while I slept she came and took my child from me, and laid her own child by my side. And when I woke, and went to feed my child, it was dead. And I knew it was not my son.

It is your son.

It is not; the child that lives is mine.

The dead child is yours.

THE JUDG-MENT OF SOL-O-MON.

In this way they spoke, and the king heard them, and said, Bring me a sword!

And a sword was brought to him.

And the king said, Cut the live child in two, and give half to one and half to the other.

When the real moth-er of the child heard these words she cried out, O my lord, give her the child, but do not kill it.

But the oth-er said, Cut it in half, and let it not be hers or mine.

Then the king told his men to give the child to the one who tried to save its life, for he knew that she was the moth-er. And it was to find this out that he sent the men for the sword, and not to take the child's life.

SHIPS OF SOL-O-MON.

When Sol-o-mon had been king for four years,

he laid out the plan that Da-vid had made for the house of the Lord.

He had a talk with Hi-ram the king of Tyre, and told him that it was time to build the house. And the king of Tyre was glad, and did all he could to aid him. He sent Sol-o-mon great trees from the woods, and sent him men to help in the work; men who had skill with the ax, and with fine tools of all sorts.

The house was built of stone, and each stone was hewn from the rock, cut so as to fit in the wall ere it was brought to the place where it was to stand, so that no ax nor tools should be used in the house when it was put up.

The walls of the rooms were in-laid with gold, and gems, and the floor of the place where the ark was kept was of pure gold, and in front of the shrine were loops and chains of fine gold.

The doors of the house were made of the wood of the fir tree, and they were carved with great skill, and touched up with gold.

It took Sol-o-mon sev-en years to build the house of the Lord; and when it was done he made a feast, and the priests brought the ark of the Lord from Mount Zi-on, where Da-vid kept it.

And all the tribes of Is-ra-el came to Je-ru-sa-lem, that they might be there when the ark was brought.

THE QUEEN OF SHE-BA DOES HOM-AGE TO SOL-O-MON.

SOL-O-MON FALLS INTO I-DOL-A-TRY.

And when the ark was put in its place, and the priests came out, there was such a cloud in the house that all stood still. For the Lord was in the cloud.

Then Sol-o-mon stood up, and with raised hands asked him to come down and dwell in the house, and to dwell in men's hearts, that they might walk in the right way, and love God all their days.

Now the fame of Sol-o-mon came to the ears of a rich queen, who dwelt at She-ba, and she thought she would like to see if this man was as wise and rich as he was said to be. She

QUEEN OF SHE-BA.

had a long way to come, and a great train came with her, and these brought loads of rich spice, and gold and sil-ver and gems of worth. And the queen had a talk with Sol-o-mon and he told her all she ought to know.

And she said to the king, What I had heard of thee in my own lands I did not think could be true. So I came to see for my-self, and I find the half was not told me. So she gave rich gifts to Sol-o-mon, and he gave rich gifts to her, and the queen went back to her own land.

Now it was thought no sin in those days for a man to have more than one wife. And some of Sol-o-mon's wives had been brought up to serve false gods. And it was a sin for the king to wed with such. And as he grew old these wives made him serve their Gods, and turn from the true God whom he had been taught to love and fear.

And this did not please the Lord, and he said that Sol-o-mon's son should not be king when Sol-o-mon died. For Da-vid's sake he would let him be a prince of two tribes all the days of his life. But ten tribes he would take from him.

And foes rose up to plague Sol-o-mon, and for his sins he had to give up the peace and rest that had long been his. When he had been king for two-score years Sol-o-mon died, and his fame has come down to this day, for no man has been born in-to the world so wise and great as King Sol-o-mon.

ELIJAH

A-hab was the last of the six kings who ruled the ten tribes. And he made them serve Ba-al, and built a house for this false god.

These acts did not please God, so he sent E-li-jah, a seer, to tell A-hab that for years and years there should be no rain in the land. And he told E-li-jah to hide near a brook from which he should drink, and the birds of the air would bring him food to eat.

E-li-jah did as the Lord told him, and he drank from the brook, and the birds brought him his food from day to day. But as there was no rain, the brook dried up, and there was lack of food in the land.

So the Lord told Elijah to go to the town of Za-re-phath, where a wo-man dwelt who would give him food.

And when E-li-jah came to the gate of the town, a poor wo-man drew near him to pick up some sticks. And he said to her, Bring me a drink, I pray thee.

And as she went, he said, Bring me, I pray thee, a bit of bread in thine hand.

E-LI-JAH FED BY RA-VENS.

And she said, As the Lord lives, I have no bread in the house, and but a hand-ful of meal, and a few drops of oil. And I came out to pick up a few sticks that I might light the fire, and bake a small loaf for me and my son, that we may eat it and die.

E-li-jah said, Fear not; go and do as thou hast said. But first make me a small loaf, and then make one for thee and thy son. For thus saith the Lord, The meal shall not waste, nor the cruse of oil fail till the day the Lord sends rain on the earth.

So the wo-man went her way and did as E-li-jah told her, and there was from that time no lack of food in her house. But one day her son was ill, and he grew worse and worse, and then died.

ELI-JAH AND THE WID-OW'S CHILD.

When E-li-jah heard of it, he said, Give me thy son. And he took the child from her arms and bore him to his own room, and laid him on his bed.

And E-li-jah cried to the Lord, and said, O Lord, I pray thee let this child's soul come back to him.

And the Lord sent back the soul of the child, and E-li-jah took the boy and brought him to his moth-er.

And she said to E-li-jah, Now by this I know that thou art a man of God, and that the word of the Lord in thy mouth is truth.

For three years there had been no rain in the land, and at the end of that time the Lord said to E-li-jah, Go show thy-self to A-hab, and I will send rain on the land.

So E-li-jah went, and on the way he met with one of A-hab's head men, who loved the Lord. He knew E-li-jah, and bade him turn back, for the king would be sure to put him to death. But E-li-jah said that he would show him-self to A-hab that day. So the man told the king that E-li-jah was near, and the king came out to meet him.

And he found fault with E-li-jah, for he thought he was to blame for the lack of food, and for the long drouth.

E-li-jah told the king to have all those he ruled meet in a mass at one place. And when they came there, E-li-jah cried out to them, How long will ye turn your hearts from God?

And he told them to prove which was the true

God, Ba-al, or E-li-jah's God. And he told them to bring two young bulls, and to take the flesh of one and lay it on the wood in front of Ba-al, and he would lay the flesh of the other young bull on the Lord's al-tar. And he said, Call ye on your gods and I will call on mine, and let the God that sends down fire be the God whom we all shall serve.

And they said it was a good plan.

So they cried out from sun-rise till noon, O Ba-al, hear us! But there was no voice or sign that their god heard them.

E-li-jah said, Cry with a loud voice, for he is a god. He may be asleep, or lost in thought.

THE LIT-TLE CLOUD.

And they cried, and made a great noise, and at last fought with their knives till they drew blood.

And E-li-jah said, Come near me.

And they all came near to him.

And E-li-jah took twelve stones, and built an altar to the Lord. And he put the flesh and the wood on it, and the wood was wet through and through.

Then he cried out, Hear me, O Lord, hear me, and let it be known that thou art the true God.

Then fire came down from on high and burnt up the flesh, and the wood and the stones, and the dust; and the ground that had been made so wet was as dry as it could be.

And when the crowd saw this they all bowed down to the ground, and said, The Lord he is God! The Lord he is God!

And they broke up the false gods, and gave their hearts for a while to the Lord.

Then E-li-jah told A-hab that he might eat and drink, for the rain would soon set in. And he went to the top of a high mount to pray for rain. Not a cloud was in the sky. The sea was calm. But E-li-jah knew that he must watch, and wait, and pray, and the sign would come.

At last there rose up out of the sea—that is, where the sea and sky seem to meet—a small cloud, the size of a man's hand. And soon the sky was black with clouds, and the wind blew, and there was a great storm of rain.

Now A-hab had a bad wife, and when he told

her what E-li-jah had done, she made a vow to kill him.

And E-li-jah had to flee for his life. He was so worn out that when he came to a lone place he sat down in the shade of a tree and wished that he might die. While he slept, an an-gel drew near, at whose touch E-li-jah woke. And the an-gel said, Rise and eat.

And E-li-jah found food and drink set out for him. And he ate and drank, and then lay down and slept. And the an-gel came once more, and bade E-li-jah eat, that he might have strength to go on his way. And he sat up, and ate the food the Lord had sent, and it gave him such strength that he

E-LI-JAH AND KING A-HAB.

went with-out food for more than a month. And at the end of that time he came to Mount Ho-reb. And he went to a cave and lay down and slept there.

And the Lord spoke to him, and said, Why art

thou here, E-li-jah? And E-li-jah said the chil-dren of Is-ra-el had not kept their word, but had gone back to their false gods, and slain all those who sought to turn them from their sins. And I have fled from them, said E-li-jah, for they seek my life.

E-LI-JAH IN THE WIL-DER-NESS.

The Lord said, Go forth, and stand on the mount. And there came a great wind that split the high hills, and broke up the rocks. But the Lord was not in the wind.

Then the earth shook, so that there was no firm ground on which to walk; and smoke came up out of the great cracks that were made. But the Lord was not in the earth-quake.

Then there came a still, small voice. When E-li-

Elijah.

jah heard it he hid his face in his cloak, and went out and stood at the door of the cave.

And the voice said, Why art thou here, E-li-jah? And E-li-jah said that he fled from those who sought to kill him. And the Lord told him to leave the cave, and go back, and pour oil on the head of E-li-sha, who was to take his place.

And E-li-jah found E-li-sha at work with the plough in a large field. And as he went by him he threw his cloak round E-li-sha.

And E-li-sha knew that this meant he must leave all and go with E-li-jah. And he went home to bid fare-well to his dear ones there, and then came back to be near E-li-jah and to wait on him.

E-LI-JAH GOES TO HEAV-EN.

Now the time drew near when E-li-jah was to leave the earth. And he and E-li-sha stood near the shore of the Jor-dan. And E-li-jah took his cloak and struck the waves, and they made a wall on each side, and the two men went through on dry land. And as they stood on the oth-er side, E-li-jah said to E-li-sha, Ask what I shall do for thee, ere I leave thee.

And E-li-sha said, Let me, I pray thee, be twice as good and wise as thou.

E-li-jah said, Thou dost ask a hard thing. But if thou dost see me when the Lord takes me from thee, then it shall be so. But if thou dost not see, then it shall not be so.

So they went on, and while they yet spoke, there came a great light in the sky, and the clouds took on strange forms. And E-li-jah was caught up as if by a whirl-wind, and E-li-sha cried out as he saw him pass through the sky, but he was soon out of sight, and E-li-sha saw him no more.

ELISHA

As E-li-jah rose from the earth he let his cloak fall on E-li-sha. And E-li-sha went down to the Jor-dan, and took the cloak and struck the waves,

Elisha.

and they stood up on each side, so that he went a-cross dry shod. And it was made known to all the seers and wise men that E-li-sha had been called to fill E-li-jah's place, and he gave proof that the Lord was with him.

As E-li-sha went from Jer-i-cho to Beth-el, some young folks ran out and made fun of him, and cried, Go up, thou bald head! Go up, thou bald head!

E-li-sha turned back, and asked the Lord to take them in hand. So the Lord sent two great bears out of the wood, and they fell on the children and tore over two-score of them.

THE CHILD-REN OF BETH-EL.

One day E-li-sha came to Shu-nem, where a rich wo-man dwelt. And she bade him come in and eat. And as oft as he went that way, he made it a rule to stop and take the food and drink she set out for him.

And she had a room built for him on the side of her house, and put a bed and a chair in it, that he might go in and out as he chose, and have a place to rest in.

And one day when he was in this room, he sent for the wo-man to come to him. And he said to her, What can I do to pay thee for all thy kind care of us? Shall I speak to the king for thee? She said there was no need, that she sought no pay, and then left the room.

E-li-sha said to his man, What is there that I can do for her?

And the man said, She has no child.

And E-li-sha said, Call her. And she came back and stood at the door. And when the man of God told her that she should have a son, she thought he did not speak the truth.

And the word of the Lord came true, for in less than a year she had a son.

And the child grew up, and went out one day to the field to see the men reap the corn. And while he was there he felt sick, and cried out to his fath-er, My head! my head!

And his fath-er said to a lad, Take the boy home to his moth-er. And she took him, and he sat in her lap till noon, and then died. And she took the boy to E-li-sha's room, and laid him on the bed of the man of God, and then went out and shut the door.

Then she sent for one of the young men, and had him bring an ass to the door, and she got on the ass, and bade the man drive as fast as he could till she told him to stop.

She went till she came near Mount Car-mel. And E-li-sha saw her, and sent Ge-ha-zi out to meet her, and to ask her if it was well with her and with the child. And she said to him, It is well.

But when she came to E-li-sha she fell at his feet, and Ge-ha-zi drew near to push her from the man of God.

But E-li-sha said, Touch her not. She is in great grief, and the Lord has hid it from me and not told me of it.

And the wo-man said, Did I ask thee for a son? Then he knew that the boy was dead.

Then E-li-sha said to Ge-ha-zi, Take my staff, and go thy way with all speed. Stop to speak to no one. And lay my staff on the face of the child.

And the moth-er of the child said, As the Lord lives, I will not leave thee. And E-li-sha rose and went with her, while Ge-ha-zi ran on a-head. And he laid the staff on the face of the child, but the child did not speak nor hear. And he ran out to meet E-li-sha and to tell him the lad did not wake.

And when E-li-sha came to the house he found the child dead, and laid on his bed. So he went in the room and shut the door, and prayed to the Lord.

Then he got on the bed, and lay on the child till his flesh grew warm. Then he left the room for a-while to walk up and down, and when he went back he lay on the child till its breath came back, and it gave signs of life.

And he sent for the moth-er. And when she came to the room he said, Take up thy son. And she fell at the feet of E-li-sha, with thanks too deep for words, and then took her son in her arms and went out.

There was a man in Sy-ri-a, who took charge of all the troops that went to war with the king. This man's name was Na-a-man, and he had done brave deeds, for which he held high rank, and was much thought of. But this man fell ill, and none but those of his own house would go near him. And there was no cure for him. But his wife had a maid to wait on her. And this maid said that if Na-a-man would go to E-li-sha she was sure that he would cure him.

And Na-a-man came down to Sa-ma-ri-a with a note from his own king to the king of Is-ra-el.

When the king of Is-ra-el read the note he was very wroth, and said, Am I God that I can bring the dead to life? For he thought that it was but a trick to bring on a war.

When E-li-sha heard that the king rent his clothes, he sent word to have Na-a-man come to him.

And Na-a-man drove up in fine style, and stood at the door of E-li-sha's house. And E-li-sha sent word to him to bathe at the Jor-dan seven times, and he would be made well.

E-LI-SHA AND THE CHILD.

This put Na-a-man in a rage, for he thought that E-li-sha would come out to him and call on the name of God, and touch him so as to heal him.

And he said, Are there not streams in Da-mas-cus in which I can bathe and be made well? And he went off in a rage.

But some of his men drew near, and said, My lord, if he had bid thee do some great thing wouldst thou not have done it? Why not then do as he says, and wash and be clean?

And Na-a-man gave heed to their words and went down to the Jor-dan. And he took sev-en baths, and then his flesh grew as soft and pink as the flesh of a child, and health and strength came back to him. And Na-a-man went back to E-li-sha's house, he and all his men, and he said, Now I know there is no God in all the earth but the God of Is-ra-el.

Now the time drew near when E-li-sha was to die. And the king, Jo-ash, came to see him as he lay sick in bed.

And E-li-sha said, Take the bow and the darts. And the king took them. And E-li-sha said, Put thy hands on the bow. And the king did so, and E-li-sha put his hands on the king's hands. Then E-li-sha said, Throw wide the east win-dow. And when this was done he said shoot. And the king shot; and E-li-sha told him that he should set Is-ra-el free from its foes.

Then he said to the king, Take the darts. And

he took them. And E-li-sha said, Strike them on the ground. And the king struck them on the ground three times, and no more.

And the man of God was wroth with him, and said, Thou shouldst have struck five or six times, for then thou wouldst have laid the Sy-ri-ans low, now thou shalt smite them but three times.

And E-li-sha died, and was laid in the ground. And one day as some of the folks

THE AR-ROW OF DE-LIV-ER-ANCE.

went out with a dead man to lay him in the grave that was dug for him, they saw a band of thieves from the land of Mo-ab and did not dare to go on. So they put the dead man in the grave where E-li-sha lay. And as soon as the corpse touched the bones of E-li-sha the man came to life and stood on his feet.

JONAH, THE MAN WHO TRIED TO HIDE FROM GOD

THERE was a seer in Is-ra-el whose name was Jo-nah. And the Lord told Jo-nah to go to Nin-e-veh, a large town where there was great need of good men. But Jo-nah did not care to go there, so he ran down to Jop-pa and found a ship there that would set sail for Tar-shish in a few days. So he paid his fare, and went on board the ship to go to Tar-shish, where he seemed to think the Lord would not find him.

But as soon as the ship was well on its way, the Lord sent forth a great wind, and the waves rose high, and the storm beat the ship, and it was blown here and there as if it were a toy. And those on board of her were in great fear, and cried out to their gods, and threw all the goods that were in the ship in-to the sea, so that she would not sink.

Jo-nah was down in the hold, where he lay and slept, though the storm was so fierce.

And the one who had charge of the ship came

to him and said, What does this mean? Rise, and call on thy God to save us from ship-wreck.

And the rest of the men said, Come, and let us cast lots that we may know who is to blame for this.

So they cast lots, and the lot fell on Jo-nah. And they said to him, Tell us, we pray thee, who has brought on us these ills. What is thy trade? where dost thou come from? where dost thou live? and of what tribe art thou?

JO-NAH IN THE STORM.

And he said I am a Jew, and have fled from the Lord who made the sea and sky.

And the men were in great fear and said, Why hast thou done this thing? And what shall we do to thee that the sea may be still for us? For the waves were rough, and the winds blew a gale.

And Jo-nah said to the men, Take me up and cast me in-to the sea; then shall the sea be calm for you, for I know it is for my sake that this great storm has come up-on you.

The men did not want to drown Jo-nah, so they tried their best to bring the ship to land, but could not.

Then they cried to the Lord, O Lord, we pray thee, count it no sin to us that we take this man's life, for thou, O Lord, hast sent this storm on us for some of his sins.

So they took up Jo-nah, and cast him in-to the sea, and the sea grew still and calm.

And when the men saw this they were in great fear, and brought gifts to the Lord, and made vows that they would serve him.

Now the Lord had sent a great fish to the side of the ship to take Jo-nah in-to its mouth as soon as he was thrown in-to the sea.

And Jo-nah was in-side the fish for three days and three nights. And he prayed to the Lord while he was in the fish; and cried to God to help him, and to blot out his sins. And God heard him, and bade the fish throw him up on the dry land.

Then the Lord spoke to Jo-nah once more, and

said, Rise, and go to Nin-e-veh, and preach to it as I bid thee.

And Jo-nah rose and went.

And when God saw them turn from their sins and pray to him, he did not do to Nin-e-veh as he said he would.

But this did not please Jo-nah. He thought that Nin-e-veh should be brought low, for those who dwelt there were not good friends to the Jews. Then, too, Jo-nah's pride was hurt, for he knew that men would laugh at him, and have no faith in what he said, so he went out of the town and sat down by the roadside.

And God made a vine to grow up there in one night, that Jo-nah might sit in its shade and find rest from his grief. And Jo-nah was glad when he saw the gourd. The next morn God sent a worm to gnaw the root of the vine, and it soon dried up.

When the sun rose God sent a hot wind, and the sun beat on Jo-nah's head so that he grew sick and fell in a faint. And he was wroth, and had no wish to live.

And God said to Jo-nah, Is it well for thee to be in such grief for the loss of a gourd?

And Jo-nah said, Yes. There was good cause why he should feel as he did and long to die.

Then the Lord said to him, Thou wouldst have

had me spare this vine which cost thee nought, and which grew up in a night and died in a night. And why should I not spare Nin-e-veh—that great town—in which are hosts and hosts of young folks who do not know their right hand from their left?

So God put Jo-nah to shame, and made him see what a sin it was to wish to crush Nin-e-veh just to please his own self and for fear men would laugh at him.

And Jo-nah found out, what we all need to learn, that it is of no use to try to hide from God.

DANIEL

There was a king of Bab-y-lon whose name was Neb-u-chad-nez-zar. And he sent one of his chief men to choose some of the young Jews who had been well brought up, that they might wait on him.

The chief chose four youths whose names were Dan-i-el, Sha-drach, Me-shach and A-bed-ne-go. And these were brought to Bab-y-lon, that they might be taught as the king wished.

And the Lord was with these four young men,

Daniel.

and made them wise, and strong in mind, and fair of face.

When they had been taught for three years they were brought to the king's house. And the king kept them near him, and made use of them, for he found that they knew ten times more than all the wise men in the whole realm.

One night the king had a dream that woke him out of his sleep. And he sent for all the wise men—those who could read stars, and those who could work charms—to tell what the dream meant.

KING NEB-U-CHAD-NEZ-ZAR.

And they all came, but none of them could tell the dream that had gone out of the king's own head. And no king, they said, would ask such a thing of wise men.

The king was wroth at this and gave word that all the wise men should be put to death. And they sought Dan-i-el and his friends, that they might kill them.

Dan-i-el said, Why is there such haste? And when he was told he went in to the king and said if he would give him time he would make his dream clear to him.

In the night God showed the king's dream to Dan-i-el, and all that it meant was made clear to him. And Dan-i-el gave praise and thanks to God who had been so good to him.

Then he went to the chief, and told him not to slay the wise men, but to bring him in to the king.

Then Dan-i-el told the king his dream, and all that would come to pass, and when the king heard it he fell on his face before Dan-i-el and said to him, It is true that your God is a God of gods, and a Lord of kings, and that nought is hid from him, since thou hast told me this dream.

And the king made Dan-i-el a great man, and gave him rich gifts, and put him at the head of all the wise men in the land.

Daniel.

Now king Neb-u-chad-nez-zar made a great god out of gold, and set it on one of the plains of Bab-y-lon.

And one of the king's men cried out with a loud voice, and said it was the king's law that all should bow down to the god of gold that he had set up. And those who did not bow down were to be thrown in-to a great hot fire and burnt up.

And some men brought word to the king that the three Jews would not serve his gods, or bow down to this one of gold which he had set up.

NEB-U-CHAD-NEZ-ZAR'S DREAM.

These three men were brought to the king, and he said to them, Is it true, O Sha-drach, Me-shach, and A-bed-ne-go that ye will not serve my gods or bow down to the one of gold which I have set up? And he said he would give them one more chance, and if they did not bow down when they heard the call, they should be cast in the same hour in-to the flames. The three Jews said to the king, Be it known to thee now that we will not serve thy gods, nor bow down to the new one thou hast set up. And if we are cast in the fire, the God whom we serve will save us from death and bring us out of thy hands, O king.

Then was the king in a great rage, and he sent word that a fierce fire should be made. And the three Jews were bound and thrown in-to the flames with all their clothes on. And the fire was so hot and they went so near that sparks flew out and killed the men who took up Sha-drach, Me-shach and A-bed-ne-go.

These three Jews fell down in the midst of the flames, but soon rose to their feet, and the Lord would not let the flames burn them.

When the king saw this he rose in great haste and said to his chiefs, Did we not cast three men bound in the midst of the fire?

And they said, True, O king.

And the king said, Lo, I see four men loose, and they walk through the flames and are not hurt, and the form of the fourth is like to the son of God.

Daniel.

Then the king came to the door of the cage of fire and said to Sha-drach, Me-shach and A-bed-ne-go, Ye who serve the most high God, come forth, and come here.

And the three young Jews came forth out of the midst of the fire, and not a hair of their head was singed, nor were their clothes harmed, nor was the smell of fire on them.

And the king praised the God who had shown that he would save from death

DWELL-ING WITH THE BEASTS.

those who put their trust in him. And the king made it a law that those who spoke ill of the God of Sha-drach, Me-shach, and A-bed-ne-go should be put to death, and their homes torn down, for there was no God who could save as he could.

For a while the king served God and gave him praise for all he had done for him. But men who thought to please the king, spoke of his great wealth and praised all that he did, so that he grew vain and proud, and thought more of him-self than he did of God.

And the king had a dream that made him shake with fear, and he sent for Dan-i-el. And Dan-i-el feared to tell the king the truth. But the king told him to speak out. Then Dan-i-el told him what would take place.

And it all came on king Neb-u-chad-nez-zar. In the same hour his mind left him and he was not fit to reign. So he was thrust out of doors, and did eat grass with the beasts of the fields. And he lay on the ground, and was wet with the dews, and his hair grew so long that his flesh could not be seen, and his nails were like bird's claws.

And at the end of the sev-en years Neb-u-chad-nez-zar raised his eyes to God, and his mind came back to him, and he spoke in praise of the most High.

And Neb-u-chad-nez-zar was made king once more, and grew strong and great, and gave the praise to God; the King of kings, who could raise up those who were down, and bring down those who were full of pride.

When Neb-u-chad-nez-zar died, a new king was

THE WRIT-ING ON THE WALL.

on the throne of Bab-y-lon whose name was Bel-shaz-zar. And Bel-shaz-zar made a great feast, and much wine was drunk. And the king sent for the rich cups which his fath-er had brought from the Lord's house in Je-ru-sa-lem. And he and all at the feast drank from these cups, which was a great sin.

In the midst of the feast there came forth a man's hand, that wrote on the wall of the king's house.

And the king saw the hand, and was in great fear, and sent at once for all his wise men.

But none of them could read what was on the wall, and the king knew not what to do. Then Dan-i-el was sent for, and the king said he should have great wealth and high rank if he could read the words on the wall.

Dan-i-el said, Keep thy gifts, O king, and give thy fees to some one else. Yet will I read the words on the wall and tell you what they mean. For the God who gives thee life and takes care of thee, thou hast no word of praise. And so God sent this hand to write on the wall.

ME-NE, ME-NE, TE-KEL, U-PHAR-SIN,

which means that thy reign as king is at an end.

When Dan-i-el had told what the hand wrote on the wall, and what the words meant, Bel-shaz-zar bade his men clothe him in red, and put a gold chain on

DAN-IEL IN THE LIONS' DEN.

his neck, and make it known that he was to be third in rank from the king.

That same night Bel-shaz-zar was slain, and Da-ri-us took his place on the throne

Now Da-ri-us was pleased with Dan-i-el, and thought him such a wise and good man that he made him chief of a large force of men who held high rank. And this made these men hate Dan-i-el, and they tried to find out some ill that he had done that they might tell it to the king. But they could find no fault in him. Then they thought of a way in which they could harm him.

They came to the king and asked him to make a law that if one should ask help of God or man for one month, he should be cast in-to a den of li-ons.

They might ask help of the king, but of no one else.

And the king told them to write down this law, and he put his name to it.

When Dan-i-el heard of the law which the king had sent out he went to his home and knelt down three times a day with his face to Je-ru-sa-lem, and gave thanks to God first as he had done all his life.

And the men who were on the watch to catch him in some crime, drew near his house and heard him pray to his God. So they went and told the

Daniel.

king, and the king was wroth to think he had made such a law. And he tried his best to save Dan-i-el. But the men held him to his word, and said it would not do for him to change a law that had been made.

Then the king bade them bring Dan-i-el and cast him in the den of wild beasts. And he said to Dan-i-el, Thy God, whom thou dost serve so well, will be sure to save thee.

And a stone was brought and laid on the mouth of the den.

ROCK GRAVE OF DA-RI-US.

Then the king went to his own house, but would take no food, nor did he sleep all that night. And at dawn he rose and went in haste to the den of wild beasts. And as he drew near he cried out with a sad voice, O Dan-i-el, canst thy God save thee from the li-ons?

And Dan-i-el said, O king, my God hath shut the li-ons' mouths so that they have not hurt me, since I had done no wrong in his sight nor in thine, O king.

CY-RUS, KING OF PER-SIA.

Then the king was glad, and bade his men take Dan-i-el out of the den. And when he was brought out, there was not a scratch found on him, for his trust was in God, and God took care of him.

Then the king had those men who found fault with Dan-i-el, thrown in-to the den—they and their wives, and their chil-dren—and the wild beasts were quick to eat them up.

Then Da-ri-us made a law that all men should serve the God of Dan-i-el, who was the one true God. When Da-ri-us died, Cy-rus was made king.

THE GOOD QUEEN ESTHER

Far back in the past, wise men had fore-told that the Jews would be kept out of Je-ru-sa-lem for three-score and ten years, and at the end of that time a king, Cy-rus, would let them go back to the land they came from. And he did so.

Not all the Jews went back to their own land, but some of them made their homes in Per-si-a and else-where. And King A-has-u-e-rus was on the throne.

In the third year of his reign he made a great feast.

And he sent for Vash-ti, the queen, to throw off her veil and let his guests see how fair she was.

But Vash-ti would not do it.

Then the king was in a rage, and said to his wise men, What shall we do to Queen Vash-ti to make her know that the king's will is her law?

And the wise men said, Vash-ti hath done wrong to the king and to all the lords of the land.

For when this is told, wives will not do as their liege lords wish. They will say, The king sent word for Vash-ti, the queen, to be brought to him, but she came not. Let the king make a law and put Vash-ti from him and choose a new queen, that all wives, great and small, may take heed and do as they are told.

The king and all the lords thought these were wise words. And the king made it a law that a man should rule in his own house.

Then some of the king's men, whose place it was to wait on him, came to him and said it would be a good plan for him to have all the fair maids in the land brought to his house, that he might choose one of them to be queen, in the place of Vash-ti.

And the king did as they said.

Now there was a Jew in the king's house, whose name was Mor-de-ca-i. He was a poor man, and was there to wait on the king.

And there was a maid named Es-ther, who was one of his kins-folk. And she was "fair of face, and full of grace."

And when the word went forth from the king, scores and scores of fair young maids came to the king's house, and Es-ther came with them. And one of the king's men had them all in his charge.

This man was so pleased with Es-ther that he was more kind to her than he was to the rest, and sent maids to wait on her, and put her and her maids

ESTHER AND THE KING.

in the best part of the house where the wo-men were. But Es-ther had not let it be known that her folks were Jews, for Mor-de-ca-i had told her not to tell it.

As soon as the king saw Es-ther he fell in love with her, and set the crown on her head, and made her queen in the place of Vash-ti.

Then the king made a great feast, and gave gifts to the poor for the new queen's sake. And she had not yet made it known that her folks were Jews.

Now two of the king's men, who stood on guard at the doors of his house, were wroth with the king and sought to kill him.

And their plot was known to Mor-de-ca-i, who was a watch-man at the king's gate. And he told it to Es-ther, and she told it to the king, and both of the men were hung. And what Mor-de-ca-i had done to save the king's life was put down in a book.

And in this same book was set down all that took place in the king's reign.

Now there was in the king's house a man whose name was Ha-man. And the king gave him a high place, and bade those of low rank bow down to Ha-man.

But the Jew at the gate would not bow when Ha-man went in and out. And the rest of the men who stood by told Ha-man of it.

Now Ha-man was a vain man, and when he saw

that Mor-de-ca-i did not bow to him as the rest did he was full of wrath. It had been made known to him that Mor-de-ca-i was a Jew.

And so he told the king if he would make a law that all the Jews should be put to death, he would give him a large sum of gold and sil-ver.

The king heard what Ha-man said, and then took his ring from his hand and gave it to Ha-man, and told him to do with the Jews as he thought best. The king gave him his ring that he might use it as a seal. And Ha-man set the scribes to work, and they wrote just what he told them, in the king's name. And when the wax was put at the end with the king's seal on it, it was the same as if the whole had been writ by the king's own hand.

Men were sent out in haste to make the law known through-out the land, that all the Jews in Per-si-a were to be slain. And when this was done Ha-man and the king sat down to drink wine.

When Mor-de-ca-i heard of the law that Ha-man had made, he rent his clothes and put on sack-cloth, and went out and cried with a loud cry. And he came and stood in front of the king's gate, though he could not pass through, for it was the law that none should pass who wore sack-cloth. And all through the land the Jews were in deep grief, so full of tears that they could eat no food; and not a few of them put on sack-cloth to show the depth of their woe.

Queen Es-ther had not heard of the law, but her maids came and told her of the state Mor-de-ca-i was in. And her grief was great, and she sent food and clothes to him, and bade the men take the sack-cloth from him. But Mor-de-ca-i would take nought from their hands, nor change his clothes.

Then the queen sent one of her head men, Ha-tach, to ask Mor-de-ca-i what was the cause of his grief, and why he had put on sack-cloth.

And Mor-de-ca-i told Ha-tach of the law that had been made, and what a large sum Ha-man had said he would give to the king if he would kill off all the Jews in the land.

And he told Ha-tach to tell the queen, and to show her what the scribes wrote, and bid her see the king and ask him to save the Jews.

And Ha-tach took the word to the queen.

Es-ther bade him tell her kins-man that it was well known that those who went in to the king when they had not been sent for, would be put to death. But if the king held out his gold wand it was a sign that he would spare their lives. The king has not sent for me for a month, said she. How then can I go to him?

Mor-de-ca-i sent back word to the queen to think

not that the king would spare her life if the Jews were put to death. And it might be that God had put her in the place she held that she might keep the Jews at this time.

Then Es-ther sent word to him that he and all the Jews in the king's court should fast and pray for her, and not eat or drink for three days and three nights.

I and my maids will do the same, said the queen, and I will go in to the king in spite of the law; and if I die, I die in a good cause.

So on the third day after the queen put on her rich robes, and went in and stood

ES-THER AT SHUS-HAN.

ve-ry near to the throne on which the king sat.

And when the king saw her, God put it in-to his heart to be kind, and he held out to her the gold wand that was in his hand. And the queen drew near, and touched the tip of the wand.

Then the king said, What wilt thou, Queen Esther? and what wouldst thou ask of me? Were it half of my realm I would give it to thee.

The queen said, If it please the king, I would like him and Ha-man to come this day to a feast I have made for them.

And the king bade Ha-man make haste, and they both went to the feast. And while they drank the wine the king told the queen to make known her wish.

But she put him off and said she would tell him the next day, if he and Ha-man would come to the feast that she would spread for them.

And Ha-man's heart was full of pride, since the queen chose him and no one else to feast with her and the king. And when he went out he felt that all men ought to bow down to him. But Mor-de-ca-i would not. And Ha-man told all his friends how kind the king and queen were to him, and what high rank he held, and said that his life would be full of joy if it were not for the Jew at the king's gate.

Ha-man's wife told him to fix a rope to a tall tree, and speak to the king the next day and have him hang the Jew. And Ha-man made a slip-noose at the end of a rope, and had the rope made fast to a tall tree.

Now that night the king could not sleep. And he sent for the book in which was put down all that took place in the realm, and had it read to him. And when he who read came to the part which told what Mor-de-ca-i had done to save the king's life, the king said, How has Mor-de-ca-i been paid for this deed?

And the man said he had had nought, and still kept watch at the king's gate.

Then the king heard a step and sent one of his men to see who it was.

Now Ha-man had come to the king's house to ask him to hang Mor-de-ca-i. And the man came back and said that Ha-man stood in the court. And the king said, Let him come in.

So Ha-man came in. And the king said to him, What shall be done to the man who has won the praise of the king?

And Ha-man thought, That means me, of course, and no one else.

And he said to the king, Let the robes be brought that the king wears, and the horse he rides, and the crown which is set on his head. And let the robes and the crown be put on the man whom the king has in mind, and bring him on horse-back through the street of the town, and have men cry out, Thus shall it be done to the man who has won the praise of the king.

And the king said to Ha-man, Make haste and take the robes and the horse as thou hast said, and do thus and no less to the Jew at the king's gate.

But Ha-man went home, and was full of shame. And he told his wife and his friends of his hard fate. And while they yet spake the king's men came for him to go to the queen's feast. And while they ate and drank, the king bade the queen make known her wish. Ask what thou wilt; were it half my realm, I would give it to thee.

Then the queen said, If it please thee, O king, take my life and spare the lives of all the Jews. For we have been sold and the truth has not been told of us, and we are to be put to death. The king said, Who is he, and where is he who has dared to do this thing?

And the queen told him it was Ha-man. And Ha-man was in great fear as he stood face to face with the king and queen.

The king rose in great wrath and went out of doors, and when he came in he saw Ha-man at the feet of the queen, where he went to beg her to save his life.

And when the king was shown the rope and the

tree on which Ha-man meant to hang Mor-de-ca-i he said, Hang *him* on it. And they hung Ha-man, and the king's wrath left him.

And on the same day the king gave Ha-man's house to Es-ther, and Mor-de-ca-i was brought in to the king, who had been told that he was a kins-man of the queen. And the king gave him the ring which Ha-man had worn, and the queen put him at the head of the house in which Ha-man had dwelt.

But Es-ther was still sad at heart be-cause of the law that had been made, that all the Jews in the land should be put to death. And she went in once more to the king—though he had not sent for her—and fell down at his feet in tears. Then the king held out the wand of gold, and the queen rose, and stood be-fore the king and asked him to change the law and save the lives of the Jews.

The king could not change the law, but he told Es-ther and Mor-de-ca-i to make a law that would please them and sign it with the king's seal. So they made a law that the Jews should kill all those who came to do them harm. And when Mor-de-ca-i came out from his talk with the king he had on a robe of blue and white, such as the king wore, and a gold crown on his head.

And all the Jews were glad; and when the day came that Ha-man had set for the Jews to be slain, the Jews went out and fought for their lives and put their foes to rout. And grief gave place to joy, and a feast was held for two days. This feast was called the Feast of Pu-rim, which the Jews keep to this day.

The Jews who had gone to Je-ru-sa-lem to build up its walls were still at work there. But there were foes to watch, and the poor Jews found fault with the rich ones, and there was strife in their midst from year to year. But when Ne-he-mi-ah went to their aid the Lord gave him strength to set things straight, and in a year the new wall was built and the gate put up. Then there was a great feast, and all the Jews gave praise and thanks to God.

But they went back to their sins, and did not serve God as they ought. And kings fought for Je-ru-sa-lem and took it from their hands and made the Jews their slaves.

And at last the Ro-mans came and took Je-ru-sa-lem and broke down its walls, and made the Jews serve them. And He-rod, who had led the Ro-mans to war, was made their king. He was a fierce, bad man, who would let no one rule but him-self. He put his own wife and two of his sons to death, and did all that he could to make folks hate and fear him.

He tried to make the Jews think that he was one of their race, but he was not. He thought it would

BUILD-ING OF THE NEW TEM-PLE AT JE-RU-SA-LEM.

BUILDING AND DEFENSE OF THE NEW CITY WALLS.

please them if he built up their House of God, so he set men to work to tear down the old and to put up the new, and they made use of much gold and sil-ver and fine white stones.

There was no ark to put in it, for that had been lost, but a large stone was put in the place where the ark should have been.

And it took He-rod more than nine years to build this House of God on the top of Mount Mo-ri-ah. And the way up to it was by a long flight of steps.

This ends the Old Tes-ta-ment, which was made up of all the books that were kept by all the scribes from the time the world was made.

Y. F. B.—16

THE WERNER COMPANY'S PUBLICATIONS.

REMINGTON'S FRONTIER SKETCHES.
By FREDERIC REMINGTON. A beautiful new pictorial, dainty in all its appointments, of highest artistic excellence. This choice collection comprises many of Remington's most notable drawings, displaying to splendid advantage his great talents and peculiar genius. 9½x13 inches. Japanese vellum binding, gilt edged, boxed. $2.00.

THE DETERMINATION OF SEX.
Schenk's Theory. By LEOPOLD SCHENK, M. D., Prof. of Embryology in the Royal and Imperial University at Vienna, and Pres. of the Austrian Embryological Institute. The last and greatest physiological discovery of the age. 12mo. Artistic cloth binding. $1.50.

THE STORY OF AMERICA.
The latest and best Young People's History of the United States. By HEZEKIAH BUTTERWORTH, for many years editor of the *Youth's Companion*, author of "Zig Zag Journeys," "The Knight of Liberty," "In the Boyhood of Lincoln," etc., etc. 8vo. 850 pages. $1.50.

SPAIN IN HISTORY.
From the days of the Visigoths, 350 A. D. to the present hour. By Prof. JAS. A. HARRISON, Prof. of History and Modern Languages at Washington and Lee University. Revised and brought down to date by G. MERCER ADAM. Large 12mo. Profusely illustrated. Emblematic buckram binding. $1.50.

CONQUERING THE WILDERNESS.
Or Heroes and Heroines of Pioneer Life and Adventure. By Col. FRANK TRIPLETT. $1.50.

BOYS OF THE BIBLE.
A book for boys of America. By THOS. W. HANDFORD Mr. Handford gives a most reverent and interesting account of the youth of our Saviour The story is one that cannot fail to inspire respect. $1.00.

THE FARMER'S ENCYCLOPEDIA.
Embracing articles on the horse, the farm, health, cattle, sheep, swine, poultry, bees, the dog, toilet, social life, etc. Size 8x5½ inches; 636 pages; green cloth binding. Price, $1.50.

FOREST AND JUNGLE.
An account of the last African expedition sent out. By P. T. BARNUM. The latest and greatest illustrated history of the animal kingdom, capture and training of wild beasts, birds and reptiles. Thrilling adventures in all quarters of the globe. Written in easy instructive form for boys and girls. 8vo., 502 pages, 84 chapters, hundreds of illustrations, large, clear type. Cloth, scarlet, stamped in black and silver. $1.50.

HOME OCCUPATIONS FOR LITTLE CHILDREN.
By KATHERINE BEEBE. What Miss Beebe's "First School Year" is to the primary teacher this little volume is intended to be to mothers. Miss Beebe believes that the ceaseless activity of children calls for employment, and "Home Occupations" is full of ways and means for mothers. Enthusiastically endorsed by the press and leading kindergartners. 75 cents.

THE PILGRIM'S PROGRESS.
New edition. Printed from new plates. Extra quality, super-calendered paper. Copiously illustrated. The most attractive Pilgrim's Progress on the market. 200 illustrations. Large quarto, 400 pages, $1.50.

For sale by all booksellers, or sent postpaid on receipt of the advertised price.

THE WERNER COMPANY, Publishers, - Akron, O.

THE WERNER COMPANY'S PUBLICATIONS.

THE WHITE HOUSE COOK BOOK.

By HUGO ZIEMAN, steward of the White House, and Mrs. F. L. GILLETTE. New and enlarged edition. $1.25.

NAPOLEON FROM CORSICA TO ST. HELENA.

De Luxe Edition. Especial attention is invited to this new and beautiful pictorial. It embodies a bird's-eye view of the life and career of Napoleon the Great. The numerous beautiful colored plates were made especially for it in France. The rich binding of royal purple, embossed in gold and white enamel, is in harmony with the other elegant appointments. Each copy is securely boxed. $4.00.

DEEDS OF DARING BY THE AMERICAN SOLDIER.

Thrilling narratives of personal daring in both armies during the Civil War. $1.50.

ILLUSTRATED HOME BOOK—WORLD'S GREAT NATIONS.

Large quarto volume. 670 pages. Scenes, events, manners and customs of many nations, with over 1,000 engravings by the most eminent artists. Present edition just published. Silk cloth, gold-stamped binding, calendered paper. $1.50.

OUR BUSINESS BOYS; OR, SECRETS OF SUCCESS.

By Rev. FRANCIS E. CLARK, Father of the Christian Endeavor movement. Small, 12mo, pebble grain, 25 cents.

"Go-at-it-ive-ness is the first condition of success. Stick-to-it-ive-ness is the second."
"If a man would succeed, there must be continuity of work."
"I have never known dishonesty successful in the long run."
"The wish for *genteel occupation* is ruinous."
"Too many young men seek soft places, and go behind the counter, when they ought to go into the field or machine shop."

MASTERS OF BRUSH AND CHISEL.

A superb selection from the world's greatest galleries and most famous private collections. Price, $1.00.

THE CROWN JEWELS OF ART.

PAINTING AND SCULPTURE. Masterpieces of artists and sculptors of all nationalities. Including all that is choicest from the World's Columbian Exhibit, the International London, Paris, Vienna, and Philadelphia Expositions. Price, $1.00.

HISTORIC MEN AND SCENES.

Portrayed by the Masters. A magnificent selection of most interesting pictures. Collected from all lands. Price, $1.00.

THE OLD MASTERS WITH THE CHILDREN.

Famous works of the world's greatest artists on juvenile subjects. Before the Judge, Cornelia and Her Jewels, Both Astonished, Crimean Gypsy Girl, Caught, Cut Finger, Christmas Box, Defiance, etc., etc. Price, $1.00.

EVERY DAY FACTS.

A complete single volume Cyclopedia for the American home. Fully up-to-date. Every Day Facts contains more than 1,000,000 facts, figures, and fancies, drawn from every land and language, and carefully classified for ready reference of teachers, students, business men, and the family circle. 485 pages; handsomely bound in paper. Price, 50 cents.

For sale by all booksellers, or sent postpaid on receipt of the advertised price.

THE WERNER COMPANY, Publishers,   -   Akron, O.

THE WERNER COMPANY'S PUBLICATIONS.

THE STORY OF CUBA.

From first to last. By MURAT HALSTEAD, veteran journalist, distinguished war correspondent, brilliant writer; for many years the friend and associate of the "Makers of History" of the Western World. There is no more graphic, incisive writer than he; no shrewder observer of men and events; no one who foretells more unerringly the trend of affairs, their sequence and conclusion. Cuba's struggles for liberty. Cause, crisis and destiny. Elegant silk-finished cloth, emblematic, ink and gold design, plain edges, $2.00; half morocco, corners tipped, gold back and center stamp, marbled edges, $2.75.

GERMANIA.

Two thousand years of German life. By JOHANNES SCHERR. Three hundred engravings. Text in German only. This famous work by the ablest of modern German historians, is a graphic narrative of the origin and grand career of the German people, a history of their religious, social, and domestic life; their development in literature, science, music, and art, and their advancement in military and political power to their present position as arbiters of the destiny of Europe. Cloth binding, ornamented in black and silver. Price, $1.00.

THE PRESIDENTIAL COOK BOOK.

The best household compendium published. Has a reputation that is national. It is based on its real worth. Every recipe it contains was actually tested by the authors and found to be invariably successful. Thoroughly up-to-date; large type; large pages plainly indexed. A handy volume. In brief, a perfect cook book. Price, 50 cents.

JOHN SHERMAN'S RECOLLECTIONS OF FORTY YEARS IN THE HOUSE, SENATE AND CABINET.

An autobiography. Being the personal reminiscences of the author, including the political and financial history of the United States during his public career. The Library Edition is issued in two royal octavo volumes containing over 1,200 pages, bound in the following styles:

Fine English Cloth, gold side and back stamps, plain edges, $7.50 per set.
Full sheep, library style, marbled edges, $10.00 per set.
Half morocco, gold center back, gilt edges, $12.00 per set.
Full Turkey morocco, antique, gilt edges, $16.00 per set.
Autograph edition, limited to one thousand numbered copies, printed on specially made paper, bound in three-quarters calf, gilt top and rough edges, imperial 8vo., boxed, $25.00 per set.

The household edition is issued in one royal octavo volume, containing about 950 pages, printed from new electrotype plates on superfine book paper, richly illustrated with carefully selected views, including places and scenes relating to the author's boyhood; also many portraits of his contemporaries in the Cabinet and Senate. In addition there are a large number of fac simile reproductions of letters from presidents, senators, governors, and well-known private citizens.

Half morocco, gold center back, marbled edges, $6.00.
Cloth, gold side and back stamp, $4.00.

MILITARY CAREER OF NAPOLEON THE GREAT.

By MONTGOMERY B. GIBBS. Not a technical military history, but a gossipy, anecdotal account of the career of Napoleon Bonaparte as his marshals and generals knew him on the battlefield and around the camp-fire. Crown, 8vo., with 32 full page illustrations. Nearly 600 pages; half green leather; gilt top and back; English laid paper; uncut edges. Price, $1.25.

For sale by all booksellers, or sent postpaid on receipt of the advertised price.

THE WERNER COMPANY, Publishers,   -   Akron, O.

THE WERNER COMPANY'S PUBLICATIONS.

THE GERMAN-ENGLISH BUSINESS LETTER WRITER.

A practical aid. Carefully prepared by competent hands, to assist in the transaction of business in either German or English. Any German with a slight knowledge of English can, with the assistance of this book, write an intelligent English business letter. The reverse is equally true. The young man fitting himself for a position requiring a practical knowledge of both German and English will find no simpler or more reliable help. Price, 35 cents.

THE QUEEN'S REIGN.

By Sir WALTER BESANT. Price, $2.50.

THE TEMPERANCE COOK BOOK.

Free from reference to ardent spirits. Over 1,100 tested recipes. Articles on carving, dinner giving, on serving, cooking for the sick, table etiquette. Good living and good health both considered. 440 pages, extra quality paper, clear type. Price, 50 cents.

GERMANY'S IRON CHANCELLOR.

By BRUNO GARLEPP. Translated from the German by SIDNEY WHITMAN, F. R. G. S., author of "Imperial Germany," "The Realm of the Hapsburgs," "Teutonic Studies," etc. The styles of binding and prices are as follows:

Fine vellum cloth, emblematic gold stamp, red edges, 475 pages, $8.00.
Half morocco, gold stamped, 475 pages, $10.00.
Full morocco, gold side and back stamps, gilt edges, 475 pages, $12.00.

THE WERNER UNIVERSAL EDUCATOR.

A manual of self-instruction in all branches of popular education. A complete cyclopedia of reference, in history, science, business, and literature. An imperial volume, 10½ inches long, 9 inches wide, and contains 830 double column pages; also one million facts and figures, one thousand forms and rules, five hundred illustrations, one hundred colored plates and diagrams, and sixty colored maps, all down to date. Half seal. Price, $5.50. Cloth, $4.00.

STREET TYPES OF GREAT CITIES.

By SIGMUND KRAUSZ. The queer people that you sometimes see as you wend your way through the crowded thoroughfares of a great city. The author has largely caught them with his camera, and we have before us snap shots, true to life, of all sorts and conditions of men. Price, $1.00.

STEAM, STEEL AND ELECTRICITY.

By JAS. W. STEELE. A new book which ought to be in every household in the country where there are young people, or their elders, who take an interest in the progress of the age. The book tells in plain, clear language the story of steam, of the age of steel, and the story of electricity. An up-to-date non-technical work for the general reader. Scientific in its facts, it is interesting as a novel. Illustrated by many pictures and diagrams. 12mo., half Russia. Price, $1.00.

MANUAL OF USEFUL INFORMATION.

A pocket encyclopedia. A world of knowledge. Embracing more than 1,000,000 facts, figures, and fancies, drawn from every land and language, and carefully classified for the ready reference of teachers, students, business men, and the family circle. Compiled by a score of editors under the direction of Mr. J. C. THOMAS, with an introduction by Frank A. Fitzpatrick, superintendent of city schools, Omaha, Neb. Full Morocco, gilt. Price, $3.00.

For sale by all booksellers, or sent postpaid on receipt of the advertised price.

THE WERNER COMPANY, Publishers, - Akron, O.

THE WERNER COMPANY'S PUBLICATIONS.

SCENIC AMERICA.

Or the Beauties of the Western Hemisphere. 256 half-tone pictures, with descriptions by JOHN L. STODDARD. Size, 11x14 inches, 128 pages. Bound in cloth with handsome side stamp. Price, **75 cents**.

PERSONAL RECOLLECTIONS OF GENERAL NELSON A. MILES.

The wonderful career of a self-made man. How he rose from a Second Lieutenant to the rank of Commander in Chief of the United States Army. Embracing the thrilling story of his famous Indian campaigns. In this volume the reader is brought face to face with the great Indian leaders: Geronimo, Crazy Horse, Sitting Bull, Chief Joseph, Lame Deer, etc. One of the most remarkable books of the century. A massive volume of 600 pages, printed on fine super-calendered paper, with nearly 200 superb engravings. Illustrated by FREDERIC REMINGTON and other eminent artists. Every page bristles with interest. An ever-changing panorama. A history in itself, distinctive, thrilling and well nigh incredible. Artistic cloth, chaste and elegant design, plain edges, **$4.00.**

THE THEORY AND PRACTICE OF TEACHING.

Presents the complete writings of DAVID P. PAGE, edited by Supt. J. M. GREENWOOD, of the Kansas City Schools, assisted by Prof. CYRUS W. HODGIN, of Earlham College, Ind. This new, revised and enlarged edition of this marvelously popular work contains a fresh and exceedingly interesting life of its noted author, with portrait. 12mo., 343 pages, cloth binding. Price, **$1.50.**

THE TEACHER IN LITERATURE.

Revised edition, is a publication of exceptional merit, containing selections from Ascham, Rousseau, Shenstone, Pestalozzi, Cowper, Goethe, Irving, Mitford, Bronte, Thackeray, Dickens, and others who have written on subjects pertaining to educational work from the Elizabethan period down. To this edition Dr. B. A. Hinsdale, Professor of Pedagogy, University of Michigan, has added an exhaustive paper on the history of the schoolmaster from earliest times as he appears in literature. 12mo. 447 pages. Price, **$1.50.**

MAGNER'S STANDARD HORSE AND STOCK BOOK.

A complete pictorial encyclopedia of practical reference for horse and stock owners. By D. MAGNER, author of the Art of Taming and Training Horses, assisted by twelve leading veterinary surgeons. Comprising over 1,200 pages. Containing over 1,750 illustrations. The finest and most valuable farmer's book in the world. Cloth binding, **$4.00**; half Russia, **$5.50.**

MARTIAL RECITATIONS.

Collected by JAS. HENRY BROWNLEE. A timely book. Martial recitations, heroic, pathetic, humorous. The rarest gems of patriotic prose and poetry. Non-sectional, enthusing. 12mo; 232 pages; large, sharp type; excellent paper; silk cloth binding, gay and attractive. Price, **$1.00**; the same in handsome paper binding, **50 cents.**

PRACTICAL LESSONS IN SCIENCE.

By Dr. J. T. SCOVELL, for ten years Professor of Natural Science in the Indiana State Normal School. Price, **$1.50.**

WOMAN, HER HOME, HEALTH AND BEAUTY.

A book that every lady should study and every household possess. An intensely interesting chapter on girlhood. Education of women. A very practical chapter on general hygiene, including hygiene of the skin and hygiene of the digestive organs. Sympathetic articles on motherhood and the hygiene of childhood. Also hygiene of the respiratory organs, hygiene of the eye, hygiene of the ear, hygiene of the generative organs. Cloth, **75 cents**; paper, **50 cents.**

For sale by all booksellers, or sent postpaid on receipt of advertised price.

THE WERNER COMPANY, Publishers,   -   Akron, O.

THE WERNER COMPANY'S PUBLICATIONS.

PRACTICAL LESSONS IN PSYCHOLOGY.

By WM. O. KROHN, Ph. D., Professor of Psychology and Pedagogy in the University of Illinois. Price $1.50.

KINGS OF THE PLATFORM AND PULPIT.

A hundred anecdotes of a hundred famous men,—our eminent orators, wits and sages. Who they are. How they have achieved fame. Their ups and downs in life,—Artemus Ward, Henry Ward Beecher, Josh Billings, John B. Gough, Petroleum V. Nasby, Robert J. Burdette, Dwight L. Moody, Robert G. Ingersoll, Bill Nye, Robert Collyer, Danbury News Man, T. DeWitt Talmage, Eli Perkins, Sam Jones, Geo. W. Peck, Wendell Phillips, Mrs. Partington, Prof. David Swing, Archdeacon Farrar, Bill Arp, etc. Large octavo volume, 7x10 inches ; 600 pages ; full of illustrations ; fine paper ; large, clear type ; attractive binding. Cloth, plain edges. Price, $1.50.

LITTLE FOLKS' LIBRARY.

A set of six instructive and vastly entertaining midget volumes, written expressly for this library by carefully chosen authors. Illustrated by noted artists. Each book contains 128 pages, and from twenty to thirty-three full-page illustrations. The books are bound in Skytogan, are sewed, and have the appearance of "old folks" books in miniature.

RHYME UPON RHYME.

Edited by AMELIA HOFER, ex-president Kindergarten Department of National Educational Association. Illustrated by Harry O. Landers, of the Chicago *Times* staff.

LITTLE FARMERS.

By W. O. KROHN, Ph. D., Professor of Psychology, University of Illinois. Illustrated by Wm. Ottman.

CIRCUS DAY.

By GEORGE ADE, special writer for the Chicago *Record*. Illustrated by John T. McCutcheon.

FAIRY TALES.

From Shakespeare. By FAY ADAMS BRITTON, Shakespearian writer. Illustrated by Wm. Ottman. Vol. I. The Tempest ; Vol. II. The Merchant of Venice. A Winter's Tale.

STORIES FROM HISTORY.

By JOHN HAZELDEN, historian. Illustrated by John T. McCutcheon, of the Chicago *Record* staff. Price, 50 cents per set.

BEAUTIFUL BRITAIN.

The scenery and splendors of the United Kingdom. Royal residences, palaces, castles, bowers, hunting lodges, river banks and islets, abbeys and halls, the homes of princes, views of noted places, historic landmarks and ancient ruins in the Lands of the Rose and Thistle. A magnificent collection of views, with elaborate descriptions and many interesting historical notes. Text set with emblematic borders, printed in a tint. A fine example of up-to-date printing. Large quarto volume, 11½x13½ inches, 385 pages, extra enameled paper. Extra English cloth, $4.50; half morocco, full gilt edges, $6.00; full morocco, full gilt edges, $7.50.

A VOYAGE IN THE YACHT SUNBEAM.

"Our home on the Ocean for Eleven Months." By LADY BRASSEY. The verdict of the public : "One of the most delightful and popular narratives of travel ever written. Both entertaining and instructive." For old and young alike. Size, 6x9 inches; 480 pages; many illustrations; extra quality paper. Cloth, gold stamped, $1.50; half morocco gold stamped, $2.00 ; full morocco, gold stamped, gilt edges, $2.50.

For sale by all booksellers, or sent postpaid on receipt of the advertised price.

THE WERNER COMPANY, Publishers,   -   Akron, O.

THE WERNER COMPANY'S PUBLICATIONS.

MAGNER'S STANDARD HORSE BOOK.

By D. MAGNER. The well-known authority on training, educating, taming and treating horses. The most complete work of the kind in existence; strongly endorsed by leading horse experts everywhere. Large quarto volume; 638 pages; over one thousand illustrations. Half Russia binding. Price, $2.50.

THE BIBLE FOR YOUNG PEOPLE.

In words of easy reading. The sweet stories of God's word. In the language of childhood. By the gifted author, JOSEPHINE POLLARD. Beautifully illustrated with nearly two hundred fifty striking original engravings and world-famous masterpieces of Sacred Art, and with magnificent colored plates. *The Bible For Young People* is complete in one sumptuous, massive, nearly square octavo volume, of over five hundred pages. Bound in extra cloth, ink and gold sides and back. $1.50.

GLIMPSES OF THE WORLD.

Hundreds of full-page views. Portraying scenes all over the world. The views composing this superb volume are reproduced by the perfected half-tone process from photographs collected by the celebrated traveler and lecturer, JOHN L. STODDARD, by whom the pictures are described in graphic language. In Glimpses of the World is presented a grand panorama of England, Scotland, and Ireland, France, Germany, Russia, Austria, Turkey, Italy, Spain, Asia, Africa, and North and South America. Unquestionably the finest work of the kind ever printed. Buckram. Price, $4.50.

THE WERNER POCKET ATLAS OF THE UNITED STATES.

A real pocket atlas 5x3½ inches, 96 pages, leatherette covers. Needed by every traveling man. Should be on every desk. Price, 10 cents.

THE CAPITOL COOK BOOK.

448 pages, 8½x6 inches; weight, 1½ pounds; over 1,400 tested recipes by HUGO ZIEMAN, ex-steward of the White House, and the well-known expert, Mrs. F. L. GILLETTE. Illustrated. Price, 50 cents.

THE WALDORF COOK BOOK.

By "OSCAR" of the Waldorf. The most thorough and complete treatise on Practical Cookery ever published. The author, OSCAR TSCHIRKY, Maitre d'Hotel, The Waldorf and Astoria, is acknowledged to be one of the foremost culinary authorities of the world. Elaborate directions are given for making ice creams, ices, pastries and tea and coffee. Selections may be made to gratify any taste. Original and varied recipes are given for making toothsome confections, preserves, jams, pickles and other condiments. Over 900 pages. Valuable information, indispensable to families, hotels, cafes and boarding houses. Wholesome, palatable, economic and systematic cooking. Everything used as food is fully considered. Nearly 4,000 recipes. The best and most comprehensive cook book compiled. Special features, such as suggestions with regard to the kitchen, menus, bills of fare, the seasons, market, etc., etc. Size, 8x10½ x 2¾ inches. Bound in one large octavo volume of over 900 pages in handsome oil cloth. Price, $2.50.

THE STORY OF AMERICAN HEROISM.

As told by the Medal Winners and Roll of Honor men. A remarkable collection of thrilling, historical incidents of personal adventures during and after the great Civil War. Narratives by such heroes as Gen. LEW WALLACE, Gen. O. O. HOWARD, Gen. ALEX. WEBB, Gen. FITZHUGH LEE, Gen. WADE HAMPTON. A war gallery of noted men and events. A massive volume of over 700 pages, printed on fine calendered paper. Illustrated with three hundred original drawings of personal exploits. English cloth, emblematic design in gold and colors, $2.50.

For sale by all booksellers, or sent postpaid on receipt of the advertised price.

THE WERNER COMPANY, Publishers, - Akron, O.

www.ingramcontent.com/pod-product-compliance
Lightning Source LLC
Chambersburg PA
CBHW022143160426
43197CB00009B/1411